D0985382

ABOUT CANADA
ANIMAL RIGHTS

HUMBER LIBRARIES LAKESHORE CAMPUS
3199 Lakeshore Blvd West
TORONTO, ON.   M8V 1K8

CAMPUS
...nd West
TORONTO, ON, M8V 1K8

ABOUT CANADA
ANIMAL RIGHTS

John Sorenson

About Canada Series

Fernwood Publishing • Halifax & Winnipeg

HUMBER LIBRARIES LAKESHORE CAMPUS
3199 Lakeshore Blvd West
TORONTO, ON.   M8V 1K8

Copyright © 2010 John Sorenson

All rights reserved. No part of this book may be reproduced or transmitted in any form by any means without permission in writing from the publisher, except by a reviewer, who may quote brief passages in a review.

Editing: Brenda Conroy
Cover design: John van der Woude
Printed and bound in Canada by Hignell Book Printing

Mixed Sources
Product group from well-managed forests and other controlled sources
www.fsc.org Cert no. SW-COC-003438
© 1996 Forest Stewardship Council

Published in Canada by Fernwood Publishing
32 Oceanvista Lane
Black Point, Nova Scotia, B0J 1B0
and #8 - 222 Osborne Street, Winnipeg, Manitoba, R3L 1Z3
www.fernwoodpublishing.ca

Fernwood Publishing Company Limited gratefully acknowledges the financial support of the Government of Canada through the Canada Book Fund, the Canada Council for the Arts and the Nova Scotia Department of Tourism and Culture for our publishing program.

  Canadian Heritage Patrimoine canadien   The Canada Council for the Arts Le Conseil des Arts du Canada   NOVA SCOTIA Tourism and Culture

Library and Archives Canada Cataloguing in Publication

Sorenson, John, 1952-
About Canada : animal rights / John Sorenson.

Includes bibliographical references.
ISBN 978-1-55266-356-1

1. Animal welfare–Canada. 2. Animal rights–Canada. I. Title.

HV4768.S67 2010   179'.30971   C2010-900017-X

CONTENTS

This book is dedicated to Lucky, Shadow, James and Bee

1. ANIMALS AND SOCIAL JUSTICE

"The greatness of a nation and its moral progress can be judged by the way its animals are treated." — attributed to Mahatma Gandhi[1]

A Civilized Society?

Canadians may think they are doing pretty well according to Gandhi's criterion. Most Canadians believe we should respect animals and treat them humanely. Over half of us have pets, many enjoy observing wildlife, humane societies operate across the country, and numerous churches conduct an October "Blessing of the Animals" (Pet Friendly Canada 2005). Prior to the 2008 federal election, both the Canadian Federation of Humane Societies and the World Society for the Protection of Animals sent the five major political parties questionnaires about anti-cruelty legislation and animal welfare. Apart from the Conservatives, who opposed legislation and refused to respond, all expressed support for animal welfare. Even those who use animals for food, clothing or in research claim to be concerned for their welfare and to observe rigorous standards. It appears that animals matter to Canadians and that we care about what happens to them.

However, Canadians seem to be affected by what Rutgers University law professor Gary Francione (2000) calls moral schizophrenia: confused and incoherent ideas about animals. While claiming to take animals' interests seriously, we regularly ignore those interests and subject animals to suffering, pain and death for trivial reasons. Clearly, our conceptions of what constitutes ethical or humane treatment are confused. We have reached a place where words lose their meaning when those who exploit, abuse and kill animals can claim to "love" them and to treat them with "respect." What does happen to animals in Canada? How much "greatness" or "moral progress" have Canadians achieved in our treatment of animals?

Although most Canadians think animals should be "treated with respect" and that "they should not be subjected to unnecessary cruelty," serious examination reveals a very different, much darker picture. But even suggesting such an examination creates problems. Questioning our treatment of animals or mentioning animal rights, veganism or even vegetarianism provokes resistance and ridicule. This hostility is shaped by massive propaganda efforts and advertising from multi-billion-dollar industries, such as meat, dairy and egg operations, restaurant and grocery chains, biotechnology and pharmaceutical corporations, research institutions and entertainment and fashion enterprises, all of which present animal exploitation as normal and acceptable, as "common sense." Opposition to animal rights is understandable from industries based upon animal exploitation. More surprising is opposition to serious thinking from those who are otherwise progressive but who ignore animal rights as a social justice issue. Some reject animal rights as sentimentalism. Many try to trivialize the issues. Dismissing concern for animals, they say human problems must be solved first. Of course, Canadians face many challenges — environmental degradation, economic turmoil, impoverishment of the Indigenous population, homelessness, threatened social services, war in Afghanistan and so on. However, caring about animals does not exclude concern for human problems. Placing these in opposition is merely a means to avoid inconvenient modifications to one's own behaviour while preserving a complimentary view of oneself as a moral person. Becoming vegan, not using animal products for clothing and boycotting circuses, rodeos and zoos are simple measures one can undertake to avoid harming animals; they require minimum effort and do not detract from engagement with other issues. No one would dream of raising such weak, bad-faith objections in any other context. We would consider it strange for someone to dismiss concern about, say, people being killed in Darfur because of ongoing atrocities in Congo. Often, those who raise this argument do little to help humans but simply use it as a means to invalidate concern for animals. As for accusations of sentimentalism, we do well to recall novelist Brigid Brophy's observation: "Whenever people say, 'We mustn't be sentimental,' you can take it that they are about to do something cruel. And if they add, 'We must be realistic,' they mean they are going to make money out of it" (quoted in Robbins 1998: 73).

Making money is fundamental to animal exploitation. Although all human societies exploit animals, the extent of oppression differs. Capitalism involves exploitation of animals as well as humans and the profit-motive extends suffering to a broader scale: billions of animals are killed each year in the food, vivisection, fashion, hunting and entertainment industries. Mistreatment of animals is shaped by systems of oppression that developed over time to maintain profit, privilege and power. Systematic, institutionalized oppression of animals is shaped by our power over them, our economic motives and our ideological justifications for using them (Nibert 2002). Speciesism is the ideology that legitimizes our exploitation of other animals. It is not just a preference for our own species but institutionalized oppression that serves the interests of wealthy elites; like racism and sexism, it is part of the structural social order. Speciesist prejudice towards other animals naturalizes their suffering, making it seem acceptable and marginalizing animal rights-based critiques. Psychologist Richard Ryder devised the term speciesism as the basis for moral objections to vivisection (animal experimentation), using it to define prejudice in favour of one's own species, comparable to racism and sexism.

From this perspective, using non-human animals for food, clothing, biomedical experiments, product testing and entertainment is reconceptualized as comparable to the worst atrocities committed against humans.

Socially Constructed Relationships

We tend to overlook the fact that our present relationship with animals is a social construction, not a natural or historical constant. For example, the globalized meat industry's intensive exploitation of animals means more meat is consumed now than ever before. Historically, humans were predominantly vegetarian, obtaining most food through foraging, not hunting. Hunting was unreliable, not the foundation of human survival, contrary to mythologized images of "man the hunter." As development of technology facilitated a gendered division of labour, killing animals increasingly became linked to male power and privilege, shaping unequal gender relations, increasing women's workloads and denigrating their social status. Development of agriculture and permanent settlements 10,000 years ago intensified ideas about hierarchy as well as exploitation of animals for labour and food; animals and women came to be seen as possessions, owned by men.

As production of animals for "meat" increased, so did requirements for grazing, which deprived humans of land needed to produce crops for their own consumption; historically, processes of intensified animal exploitation are linked to human hunger. While the rich hoarded food to feed animals they ate, poor humans faced starvation.

Patriarchal exploitation of animals provided a model for oppressing humans and these forms of oppression are materially and historically interrelated (Nibert 2002). Economic exploitation of animals was essential to colonialism as Europeans developed huge industries based on fur and skin trades, fishing, whaling and cattle-herding. Animals became the means to obtain greater wealth, and profits from these industries fuelled the development of industrial capitalism.

Development of capitalism intensified exploitation of those defined as lesser beings, both animal and human. Oppression of animals runs parallel to violent racism, including enslavement of Africans and attempts to exterminate Jews and other "undesirable" populations in Europe (Davis 2005; Patterson 2002; Speigel 1996), as well as to oppression of women (Kheel 2008; Luke 2007). Consistently, humans justify exploiting others of their own species by describing them as animals, who are, by definition, unworthy of ethical concern and can be subjected to any form of atrocity.

Animals and Ethics

In 1894, socialist Henry Stephens Salt became the first writer to explicitly state the case for animal rights in his remarkable book, *Animals Rights Considered in Relation to Social Progress*. An ethical vegetarian, anti-vivisectionist and opponent of blood-sports, Salt (1894: 19) argued that animals should be recognized as individuals with their own interests, that they deserved not just better treatment but, like humans, should be awarded rights since "the same sense of justice and compassion apply in both cases." Much of what Salt wrote was restated in Australian philosopher Peter Singer's *Animal Liberation*, which galvanized the modern animal rights movement. This is ironic, since Singer, unlike Salt, endorses not animal rights but welfare. Adopting utilitarian philosopher Jeremy Bentham's idea that animals' ability to feel pain requires us to give them moral consideration, Singer believes ethically correct actions are those that lead to the greatest happiness for the greatest number.

Singer believes interests should not be distinguished along the lines of species, arguing that all beings capable of suffering deserve moral consideration and that all interests should be considered equally. He compares liberation of animals with liberation of women or African Americans, in the sense that morally irrelevant physical differences (sex, skin colour, species) are unacceptable as a means of differentiating interests. Moral consideration must be based on capacity to suffer; no reason, beyond prejudice, exists for not considering other animals' interests. Although all sentient beings should have their interests considered equally, Singer does not consider all lives (including human lives) of equal value or that all beings should be treated equally. Different beings have different needs, and some rights, such as the right to vote, simply are irrelevant to non-human animals.

Singer does not think animals (or humans) have inherent rights. Emphasizing minimization of suffering, he says animals should be treated humanely but thinks they lack self-awareness, continuous mental existence and interest in continuing to live, and therefore it is all right to kill and eat them if they are killed painlessly and replaced by other animals. Essentially, Singer considers animals to be replaceable units with little consciousness. These notions are unconvincing to those who observe behaviour of companion animals and also are challenged by new work in cognitive ethology that shows animals have a much more complex mental life than we have assumed.

Singer's decision to judge actions by consequences offers little protection to animals, since he accepts harming them if some larger number of humans would benefit. Indeed, Singer's ideas put him at odds with the animal rights movement. In *Animal Liberation,* Singer endorsed vegetarianism since raising animals humanely for food on a scale to supply modern societies is economically impossible. More recently, he claimed humans can be "conscientious omnivores" by eating animals who are raised and killed "humanely" and praised corporations such as Whole Foods, suggesting that they have made significant improvements in animal welfare.

Ideas about animal rights find more support from philosopher Tom Regan (1983). Recognizing humans' basic moral right to respectful treatment, Regan extends this to other beings. Animals should not be regarded simply as resources for human use but as beings with their own inherent value whose moral status is comparable to that of humans. He opposes using animals for food, in vivisection and in clothing and entertainment industries. Regan says we should respect interests of animals who are subjects of a life, that is, those who are not merely alive but who have a complex mental life involving perceptions, desire, memory and intent. Originally, Regan applied this criterion to adult mammals but now includes other animals, acknowledging difficulty in drawing a line. Nevertheless, all subjects of a life should receive respectful treatment and not be harmed. Whereas Singer considers it ethically acceptable to kill animals "humanely" (a dubious notion), Regan rejects this. He opposes using animals regardless of any possible benefits to humans, even in what may be the strongest case, biomedical research. He believes emphasis on animal experimenta-tion prevents scientists from developing other methods that could provide comparable or superior results. Nevertheless, Regan does not consider all lives as being of equal value, arguing that because humans have self-awareness and a sense of the future, it would be acceptable to sacrifice a million dogs to save one human.

However, Gary Francione rejects this, considering sentience the quality that endows animals with moral significance, regardless of other characteristics such as self-awareness, language or cognitive abilities. Francione says animals need one right: not to be consid-ered property. His abolitionist approach eschews all use of animals. Advocating nonviolent vegan education, Francione thinks animal rights have been undermined by neo-welfarist approaches, which claim victories through promoting larger cages, free-range eggs or humane slaughter. These approaches do little for animals and instead help to legitimize exploitation and make people more comfortable about continuing to regard animals as commodities and consum-ing them. Calling this neo-welfarism or neo-carnism, abolitionists criticize groups that claim to be advocates for animals for endorsing "humane" products that still involve exploitation and killing. Some modest gains, such as room to turn around in their cages, may have been achieved for some animals. To the extent that such measures may reduce immediate suffering, they are commendable, but a major effect of neo-welfarism is to perpetuate suffering by encouraging people to exploit and kill animals but to feel less guilty about it.

Animal Rights and Social Justice

Some think concern for animals developed only recently, reflecting sentiments of Western, urban, middle-class people disconnected from nature. In fact, ethical treatment of non-human animals has a long history in Western thought, extending back to classical Greek philosophers such as Pythagoras, Porphry, Plutarch and Empedocles. Major religions include merciful treatment of animals as an important principle, typically overlooked in practice. Christianity has been particularly hostile towards animals; just as the Church justified patriarchy and slavery, it endorsed speciesism. Christian ideology asserts that humans have dominion, which (despite minority tendencies that interpret this as caring stewardship) is typically understood to mean that animals exist to serve us and meet our needs. European philosophers shared this view; for example, Kant maintained that animals exist only for humans, and Descartes claimed animals were merely automatons who could feel no pain; therefore, we have no ethical obligations towards them.

Mobilization for animal rights is a serious social justice movement, sharing fundamental elements of other progressive political movements: a sense of compassion and fairness, a focus on power relations and a critique of domination, inequality and hierarchy, along with efforts to alleviate conditions of exploitation. Historically, animal advocates also struggled for human rights. For example, in the early nineteenth century, Elizabeth Heyrick, who opposed animal abuse in cruel sports such as bull-baiting, campaigned for immediate abolition of slavery and emancipation of slaves when most British anti-slavery organizations were taking a gradualist approach, mobilized women's involvement, including boycotts of slave-grown sugar, supported prison reforms and advocated for the homeless. Similarly, in 1824, anti-slavery activist Catherine Smithies created the Bands of Mercy to oppose hunting. Late-nineteenth century socialist Edward Carpenter, who we would today call an environmentalist and gay-rights activist, was a vegetarian and anti-vivisectionist and supported animal rights. In 1891, Henry Salt, a socialist and pacifist involved in prison and school reform, created the Humane League and campaigned for vegetarianism and against hunting, vivisection and other forms of animal exploitation, linking these with human exploitation. Consistently, animal rights advocates supported women's emancipation and feminism, anti-slavery, anti-racism and civil rights, and anti-war activism. Many, like Ronnie Lee, a founder of the Animal Liberation Front (originally named the Band of Mercy after Smithies' group) were influenced by socialist and anarchist politics. What is remarkable about the animal rights movement, however, is that it exceeds other social justice movements by extending compassion and concern beyond the boundaries of our own species.

David Nibert (2002) notes that animal rights theorists tend to focus on ethical dimensions of speciesism, but Nibert argues that it is critical to recognize economic and institutional structures underlying this system of exploitation and how animal oppression is entangled with human oppression. Ecofeminists, who propose an ethic of care based on compassion, analyze animal exploitation in conjunction with other types of oppression, particularly that of women (Donovan and Adams 2007). For example, Adams (2000) analyzed links between exploitation of animals and pornography, images of animals and women as objects to be consumed, often depicted in violent conflation of sex and death. Considering oppressions of class, gender, racism and species as mutually supporting expressions of patriarchy, ecofeminists propose a holistic approach to interconnected issues of animal advocacy, environmental ethics and feminism. Although we now recognize intersecting oppressions of class, gender and racism, we are only starting to challenge our anthropocentric orientation and acknowledge speciesism as another socially constructed system of domination.

Nibert (2002) explains entangled oppressions of animals and humans by highlighting economic exploitation, power (sanctioned by states and allowing dominant groups to use violence to maintain their economic interests at the expense of the dominated) and ideological justifications. Humans exploit animals for economic benefit, making them both workers and slaves: their labour is useful to those who own them as property and their bodies are commodified, as meat, eggs, milk, fur, leather, as tools for research, as objects of entertainment and as pets. Any form of exploitation and violence against animals is socially accepted and defended by the state if it produces profits. Individual acts of sadism may be condemned if performed purely for personal pleasure, but virtually the same acts can be conducted in laboratories under the name of research and institutionalized torture and killing are accepted as standard industry practices.

All human societies have exploited animals although the extent of oppression differs. Capitalism intensifies the scale of exploitation, subjecting billions of animals to suffering and death, and expanding oppression into globalized systems of agribusiness, pharmaceutical and biotechnology industries, wildlife and pet trades, sport hunting and zoo and entertainment industries. Exploitation of animals is a fundamental component of capitalism, systematic and institutional-ized, with interlocking industries that breed, feed, cage, sell, transport, experiment upon and slaughter animals, using their skins, flesh, organs and genetic material. Industries that exploit animals directly are underpinned by subsidiary businesses that supply the materials and equipment to do so. Animals are transformed into machines and their bodies bear the marks of their exploitation through breeding, branding and butchering. Hribal (2003) considers animals part of the working class, contributing unpaid labour essential to the devel-opment of capitalism (although they have not developed the class-consciousness that human workers may adopt). Owned as property, animals are both labour, as they are forced to work to produce other commodities, and raw materials, commodities themselves, their bodies sold as food, clothing or research tools. Animals are also objectified and assigned value through entertainment spectacles such as circuses, rodeos and zoos.

All forms of oppression legitimize themselves through ideologies that justify systems of power and domination, presenting exploitation as the natural outcome of a hierarchical ranking of beings. Industries are supported by mass media and consumer culture that endorse animal exploitation through advertising and propaganda depicting animals as objects and commodities. Just as racist propaganda portrays its human victims as deserving of and, often, happy with their subordination, speciesist propaganda depicts animal exploitation as natural and acceptable, often portraying animals eagerly offering themselves for consumption. Animal exploitation is taken for granted, considered natural, just as enslavement of Africans and extermination of "lesser races" of humans were seen as inevitable in the march of progress. Treating humans like animals is a standard means to dehumanize subordinated humans and thus render them deserving of atrocities directed against them. Typically, racist discourse operates by animalizing the despised other humans and describing them as vermin, cockroaches, dogs, pigs, apes and so on, rendering them fit for enslavement or extermination.

Speciesism and animal exploitation structure our world just as legal slavery structured it in the recent past. Those who benefit from such structures of oppression proclaim them natural and find arguments to defend them. The political left shares speciesist ideas, accepting animal exploitation as natural, considering animal rights disconnected from other progressive concerns and sometimes even opposing it. Progressives claim to be motivated by compassion but, unreasonably, sharply limit it by confining concern to members of their own species. Professions of compassion are unconvincing when contradicted daily by a diet directly based upon others' misery.

Since animal products are unnecessary for survival and vegan diets healthier, consuming animal products is justified on the basis of taste or tradition. No one would accept such reasons in defence of human slavery or other forms of oppression, and they are no more acceptable when the victims are non-humans. Unnecessary suffering is something everyone claims to abhor, yet we perpetuate this against animals on the slightest of pretexts. Consuming animals because we like the taste of their flesh is no different from the sadist who blowtorches a dog; the pleasure we derive from exploiting others does not justify our actions (Francione 2000). Animals should not be treated as things, as the property of others; they are not resources or means to our ends but beings who have their own interests, and the principle of equal consideration must apply to all sentient beings. We cannot use others simply as our tools, and there are no humane forms of exploitation and murder. It is hypocritical for those who espouse other progressive causes to endorse hierarchy, oppression and exploitation simply because the victims belong to other species. Since species is not a morally relevant factor, this is no more acceptable than justifying oppression because the victims belong to other "races."

Despite widespread human exploitation, animal exploitation dwarfs it in terms of the sheer numbers of individuals involved and the suffering they endure. Animals are completely at the mercy of their owners, who can do anything to them for profit. They are made slaves and chattel for their entire lives, forced to work for their owners and are treated worse than human workers, who, despite countless degradations, are not usually killed and eaten or skinned for clothing. The unacceptability of these violations is reflected in the outraged cry of virtually every human group that feels they have suffered impossible indignities and unbearable atrocities: "we were treated like animals!"

Like other social justice movements animal rights is a critique of power, hierarchy and inequality and an attempt to eliminate them. However, animal advocacy surpasses other movements by extending concern and compassion beyond boundaries of species. This is based on a principle of equality, which means animals' interests should receive equal consideration with human interests. Obviously this does not mean that all have the same interests, so it is not necessary to treat all the same way. Mark Rowlands (2002) suggests a simple method of deciding what is equitable and just. Adapting John Rawls' idea of an original position, Rowland suggests we must conceive of a just society without knowing what role we will play in it. Removing all morally irrelevant variables such as class, gender, racial categorization

— and Rowlands includes species as one of these morally irrelevant features — the rational choice is to devise a society in which things are divided fairly and evenly, so we are more likely to design a world that is better for all.

Note

1. Although this quote is widely attributed to Gandhi, no source is supplied. The International Vegetarian Union, which Gandhi joined in 1890, suggests that although Gandhi may have expressed the idea, it originated in his friend Howard Williams' 1882 collection *The Ethics of Diet: A Catena*. Williams quotes Dr. David Strauss (*Die Alte und die Neue Glaube*) "The manner in which a nation, in the aggregate, treats the other species, is one chief measure of its real civilisation." Gandhi mentions the book in his autobiography and may have shared its view (International Vegetarian Union n.d.).

2. FUR AND FEATHERS

Animals, Economics and Identity

Animals are central to Canada's history, objects of economic, political and ideological struggle. Although some scientists think hunting caused extinction of many large mammals in North America during the Pleistocene period, about 11,000 years ago, Indigenous societies generally learned that overhunting threatened their own interests. They practised what we would now term "sustainable resource management," reinforced through cultural ideas of respect for animals. European attitudes toward animals were shaped by Biblical assertions that humans had "supernaturally granted" dominion over other animals, widely interpreted as legitimizing every form of exploitation. Whereas Indigenous cultures perceived overlaps, communication and transformations between humans and other animals, generally Europeans were convinced of absolute human superiority, although the situation is more complex (Preece 1999). With the development of capitalism, animals became commodities and sympathetic attitudes towards animals were overshadowed by the drive to exploit them.

European interest began with fish; early settlements in Newfoundland and Nova Scotia were established as camps to dry fish for transporting back to France and England. Europeans considered furs valuable commodities and traded with Indigenous people to obtain them. Indigenous people were numerically dominant and economically useful, helping Europeans survive and providing desired resources. The fur trade also created new cultural groups, such as the Metis, as European men, largely French and Scottish, formed relationships with Indigenous women for personal and economic reasons. These relationships provided commercial partners and kinship links that helped them to obtain furs and to survive, since women made clothing, prepared food and taught them how to live in nature. Eventually the Metis perceived a distinct identity, especially after 1820 in the Red River settlement in Manitoba, when they felt threatened by incursion of European settlers. Relationships between Metis and First Nations were strained as the bison were eradicated from the plains. As the fur trade declined, so did the Indigenous peoples' usefulness. Thus, in Canadian history, exploitation of animals is directly involved with erosion of Indigenous cultures and production of new cultural groups.

Originally, Europeans were uninterested in establishing colonial settlements in Canada but sought to extract resources, including animals' skins. Beavers' skins became the focus of European interest, and the beaver became Canada's national symbol, figuring on the first postage stamp, issued in the colonies in 1849, on the nickel coin in 1937 and as the symbol of Montreal's 1976 Summer Olympics. On U.S. President Barrack Obama's first official visit to Canada in 2009, he selected a Beaver Tail pastry at Ottawa's Byward Market. The beaver's qualities make it an interesting national symbol. The world's second-largest rodent (after the capybara), beavers are industrious, hard-working engineers, who form close-knit family groups. Although their dams can cause floods that threaten other species, they play important and beneficial roles in the ecosystem. For example, globally, there is a worrisome decline in numbers of amphibians, but University of Alberta researchers in 2007 showed that beaver ponds play a major role in preserving these other species (Stevens, Paszkowski and Foote 2007).

However, Europeans had little interest in beavers themselves, seeing them only as raw materials. From about 1550 until 1850, felt hats were fashionable, and beavers' fur was the most desirable material for producing them. By the late 1500s, the beaver was extinct in western Europe and nearly so in Scandinavia and Russia. North American beavers were a new source of furs, and the hat industry became the driving force of the fur trade, encouraging westward expansion. Europeans paid high prices for beaver hats until the mid-nineteenth century, when silk hats became fashionable. Changes in style left the Hudson's Bay Company with a surplus of beavers' skins that it could not sell to London markets, although demand continued for the fur of other animals such as bison and martens.

Industry Propaganda: Indigenous People

Acquiring animals' skins required Europeans to establish political and economic relationships with Indigenous peoples, changing their societies forever. First Nations people were co-opted into the system nearly at the lowest level, trapping animals to provide skins to satisfy European desires. Of course, animals were at the very bottom of the system: they were killed for fashion.

Industry propaganda says trapping animals for their fur preserves First Nations culture and tradition; thus, the Fur Council of Canada (FCC) presents itself as a defender of Indigenous society. However, it is silent about major threats to First Nations such as tar sands industrial projects that poison their environment and spread cancer through their communities. The FCC uses First Nations people as marketing tools, and its 2007 advertising campaign presents fur as a "green" product, as if killing animals and treating their skins with a variety of toxic chemicals to produce clothing for wealthy elites were environmentally friendly. People for the Ethical Treatment of Animals (PETA) (n.d.a) notes:

> According to Statistics Canada, only 3% of all fur available for sale in North America comes from native trapping.

Making an average of $225 per year from the sale of animal skins, aboriginal trappers are paid a pittance for doing the dirty, exhausting, bloody work of an industry that cares nothing about the indigenous people and even less about the animals. While the fur industry claims that aboriginal survival depends on trapping and the sale of fur, clearly, the continuation of trapping as the sole source of income will keep aboriginal people below even subsistence-level incomes.

Concerning industry claims, this so-called "tradition" of trapping animals to sell their fur as commodities is only a few centuries old. Indigenous people work in that system at low levels, and the fur trade represents the beginning of the end of Indigenous autonomy and of their identity. Some Indigenous people challenge industry claims to support tradition. Rod Coronado (2000), an Indigenous activist imprisoned in the U.S. for destroying commercial fur farms, stated:

As an indigenous person, the fur trade represents so much more to me than just animal abuse. It represents cultural genocide. They were the foot soldiers of an invasion and conquest in the "new world."... I have an incredible empathy with the animals that are on fur farms and in the wild in steel-jaw leg hold traps because they are my relations and they are suffering just as my ancestors suffered. And the fur trade today is the modern incarnation of those very same people who murdered and destroyed my people and my homelands.

Similarly Paul Hollingsworth (1990), Ojibway founder of the Native/Animal Brotherhood and consultant to Toronto's Animal Alliance, describes how the fashion industry contradicts traditional Native values:

Fashion fur is not the Native way. Native tradition calls for the economical and respectful use of animals. No traditional Native would dream of killing 40 small animals to create a piece of clothing that one large animal would provide. Being forced to kill is an act distasteful to any of us and to kill for such a trivial reason as to make a fur coat is horrible indeed.

Hollingsworth identifies the Canadian government's deliberate decision, in the "Public Opinion Manipulation" section of its document *Defence of the Fur Trade*, to use concern for First Nations people as industry propaganda and to accuse the anti-fur movement of cultural genocide. Describing Native people as the fur industry's tools, Hollingsworth denounces the hypocrisy and opportunism of promoting subsistence-level jobs like trapping while cutting education programs that could provide alternatives:

> They continue to promote the myth that trapping is culturally and economically central to Canada's Natives. This policy results in the illusion of concern for Native Canadians while poverty, inadequate housing, social services, daycare and education are met with cutbacks to federal economic development programs and a refusal to recognize Native land claims and the right to self government.

The FCC claims Native people depend on trapping, yet only 5 percent of the Aboriginal population is involved in trapping, only 1 percent of money generated by the trade goes to Aboriginal trappers, only 3 percent of pelts sold in North America are supplied by them and the average trapper's net income from this activity is only $225 (Global Action Network n.d.) Rather than keeping a few people engaged in brutal activities that provide little income, more efforts should go towards resolution of self-government and problems of poverty and suicide. Industry claims of concern for First Nations people should be read with these points in mind.

Profits and Doublespeak

While First Nations trappers earn little, others profit. Statistics Canada says the value of "wildlife pelts" decreased 17.9 percent to $25.8 million in 2006–2007 compared with 2005–2006, despite increased quantity from 942,596 to 1,047,428, about 11 percent. Pelts from ranch-raised animals increased from 1,652,230 pelts in 2006 to 1,806,050 in 2007, valued at $115.5 million, up 28.1 percent. Over 85 percent of Canadian fur manufacturing is based in Montreal; Toronto accounts for almost all the rest. About 90 percent of Canada's fur garment exports go to the U.S., followed by European and Asian markets. However, the International Fur Trade Federation (IFTF) reported global sales for fur clothing of $15 billion in 2007 — up 11 percent from 2006, continuing a decade of growth, reflecting not only "luxury markets" in China and Russia but the conviction of "luxury consumers" generally that they could now "feel good about" their purchases, following intensive propaganda efforts portraying the industry as committed to animal welfare, environmentally conscious and supportive of Aboriginal communities. Like all animal exploitation industries, the IFTF claims animal welfare is "paramount," an obvious falsehood in an industry based on killing animals and tearing off their skins.

Industry doublespeak not only transforms exploitation into welfare but changes hideous tortures into elegance and sophistication. Advertisers portray fur as a luxury product worn by glamorous people. Through advertising's magic system, in which commodities' social meanings are transferred onto their owners, female models are identified with animals whose skins they wear, often using sexual imagery. Animalization of women represents both as commodities, and since the animals are killed, the chain of associations is bizarre. Rather than representing glamour and elegance, the fur trade is a gruesome business, and those who wear or admire these products demonstrate more than anything else their insensitivity and callous disregard for millions of animals.

Industry Propaganda: Humane Killing

Although the fur industry portrays itself as humane, its tools are gruesome. Some devices trap animals alive by snaring their limbs or holding them in a box; others are designed to kill, by choking animals or breaking their necks. However, animals may not enter traps as designed or the impact may not be sufficient to kill them. Some die slowly as they struggle to pull a broken leg from a steel-jawed trap or try to escape by biting off the limb. Others die of blood-loss, starvation, dehydration or gangrene. Animals trapped in water may drown. Those captured alive face a brutal death. To avoid visible wounds that reduce prices of the animals' fur, trappers strangle them, club them to death or stamp on their chests.

Leg-hold traps are banned in many countries but still widely used in Canada. Recognizing their cruelty, in 1991, the European Union outlawed leg-hold traps and banned imports of fur from countries using them. Rather than supporting such modest reforms, Canada undermined them. First, Canada went to the GATT, citing unfair impositions on industry. When negotiations failed, in 1997, Canada developed the Agreement on International Humane Trapping Standards. Adopted in 1999, this allowed Canadian fur imports to continue and slightly modified traps to be used, now called "restraining" devices and presented as "humane." Leg-hold traps are still used for certain animals on land and semi-aquatic animals in water (but they kill indiscriminately), so the agreement did little to reduce cruelty, but, by spending millions of taxpayers' dollars, the Canadian government helped the industry evade attempts to regulate its practices.

The government and the IFTF invested over $13 million to develop "humane traps," essentially funding the industry to help it subvert an international agreement that might have modified some forms of animal suffering. Much of this money went to the Alberta Research Council, which tested various devices on animals, and the Fur Institute of Canada boasts that this "places Canada as the world leader in trap research." The new "humane" trapping procedures began in 2007.

Although the industry creates horrible suffering for animals trapped in the wild, most fur is taken from animals raised on industrial fur farms that confine thousands of animals. As with other forms of animal exploitation, the fur industry governs itself, establishing voluntary codes of practice that are mainly public relations tools. Animals spend their lives in filthy pens, prevented from carrying out normal functions, and sometimes can barely move. Since the object is an undamaged pelt, fur farmers devised various means to kill them at the end of their miserable existence: anal electrocution, breaking their necks, clubbing them, gassing them or injecting them with poison. Every fur coat is made of dozens or, depending on species and size, even hundreds of individual animals, each of whom experienced unique suffering.

The FCC's "Set the Record Straight" propaganda campaign asserts "Fur is Green," describes fur as "a renewable resource" and says that through "careful management, there are probably as many beavers in Canada today as when Europeans first arrived." In fact, beavers were almost driven to extinction and only survived because tastes shifted to silk hats. Use of such "green" or "environmentally friendly" terminology in advertising is unregulated, so even the most destructive and polluting industries can claim concern for the environment. Industry propaganda depicts a lone trapper on snowshoes, but most fur is factory farmed and even taking animals from the wild involves various vehicles to monitor traplines that may cover hundreds of square kilometres and to transport corpses. The industry presents its products as organic but extremely carcinogenic chemicals are used in bleaching, tanning and dyeing skins; these chemicals pollute soil and water in surrounding areas, as does waste from animals penned in fur farms. To prevent skins from rotting, they are treated with preservatives, and, even then, the industry cautions that furs should be stored in refrigerated vaults during hot weather, requiring increased energy costs. A chemical-intensive, polluting industry that violently extracts millions of animals from their habitat cannot be described as environmentally friendly. In addition to animals who are targeted for their fur, traps also kill others, such as birds and wandering pets, as well as endangered species, who are simply tossed aside as trash. For example, CBC News (2008a) reported Natasha Swan's shock at finding her cat Lenny, who had wandered from her Saskatoon home, gasping for air and in pain with the jaws of a leg-hold trap clamped around his abdomen.

Ecological consequences of killing large numbers of animals year after year and related impacts on other species are unknown. Despite industry claims to be effective managers of wildlife, trappers try to kill as many animals as possible, to make more profits. Limited staff, budget cuts and government deregulation mean there is almost no enforcement of any laws that do exist to oversee trapping. Historically, industries based on animal exploitation have not "harvested animal resources sustainably" but instead have driven those animals into extinction while pursuing short-term profits.

The FCC's "Environmental Activist!" advertisement shows a young fur-clad woman in a tree and claims that wearing fur "protect[s] nature by supporting people who live on the land [who will] sound the alarm [when] vital wildlife habitats are threatened." Another advertisement, "Cree Trapper's Message," repeats the industry's myth of supporting Native people, showing an Aboriginal man cooking an animal and asking: "When his family has eaten the beaver roast… should he throw away the fur?" Most Aboriginal communities do not depend on hunting or trapping for subsistence but do so to supplement their income or food supply. As noted, only a miniscule percentage of the industry's huge profits goes to Native trappers. The industry does not care about Aboriginal communities but uses them to deflect attention from and defend the interests of those who make the greatest profits.

The advertisement appeals to Canadians' common sense by assuring them that "Nothing is wasted." It tries to establish common ground and naturalize animal exploitation: "Most of us eat steak and hamburger. So it makes sense to use leather that cows also provide." Under the logic of capitalism, in which life is merely a commodity, it does "make sense" to exploit all animals. However, a more ethically developed consciousness informed by animal rights recognizes that since it is unnecessary either to eat animals or wear their skins to survive, both are a waste of those animals' lives as well as those of millions of other animals who are not targeted for their skins but are caught accidentally. Although the fur trade is part of Canada's history, by now we should have evolved enough morally to abandon these barbaric practices.

Industry Propaganda: Tradition

Cultural traditions are frequently invoked to legitimize animal exploitation. For example, the British Army's Queen's Guards persist in using Canadian black bears' fur for their gigantic helmets. Throughout history, killing animals and displaying or wearing their body parts have been means to signify imperial power and masculine identity, and the military is reluctant to give up such symbols. However, army representatives justified rejecting calls for synthetic alternatives by saying these lack the "lustre" of real fur. In the *National Post* (September 2, 2008), Kevin Libin applauded the "200-year-old tradition and perhaps one of the most recognizable material symbols today of Britain's historic might and glory." (Libin also cheered Kentucky Fried Chicken's traditions and "reassuring... conservatism, where... chickens would be prepared with neither mercy nor heed to the animal rights lobby" and disparaged PETA's concern for "so-called 'abuses' as 'cutting their throats while they're still conscious.'") The RCMP also defends their traditional winter hats using fur of muskrats killed in cruel leg-hold traps. Fur Bearer Defenders visited RCMP headquarters in September 2004, bringing some traps, and asked them to find a synthetic alternative. In December 2008, the RCMP's National Communications Service Webmaster responded to me by email that "informal testing" of the synthetic "confirms that it did not perform to the same level" as the fur hat. The military and the police are no friends of animals, or of animal activists, and their refusal to abandon their "traditional" hats is likely based on such animosity as well as the sexual politics of animal exploitation (Adams 2000): patriarchically rooted fears that it would be unmanly to wear synthetics when one could place a dead animal on one's head.

Other traditional practices also involve using animal body parts. In February 2009, a traditional Asian-medicine company, Wing Quon Enterprises Ltd., was fined $45,000 in Richmond provincial court for possessing and selling medicines containing parts from tigers and other endangered or protected species, including bear, pangolin, musk deer and rhinoceros. Throughout the 1990s Chinese-born Canadian geophysicist and activist Anthony Marr, of Heal Our Planet Earth, campaigned against use of endangered species in traditional Chinese medicine, rejecting magical beliefs that consuming body parts of powerful animals strengthens corresponding parts of the human body. Marr's undercover reports revealed tiger-bone pills, rhinoceros-hide, bear gall-bladders and penises of dogs, deer, tigers, seals and wolves being sold in Chinese apothecary shops in Vancouver and Toronto. Just as his campaign against bear-hunting in B.C. inspired crowds of hunters to disrupt his public lectures and issue death threats, Marr's criticism of traditional medicine resulted in accusations from the Chinese community that he would encourage negative cultural stereotypes. Noting that his criticisms would be attacked as racist if made by a White person, Marr emphasized the importance for Chinese people to speak out and to show that not all have disregard for animals.

Another example concerns traditional use of eagle feathers. After investigating eagle killings, in 2008, police charged fifteen people under B.C.'s *Wildlife Act* for trafficking in protected birds. They were participants in a network that ships eagle parts from Canada across the U.S. for use in ceremonial events. The rarity of these endangered birds led the U.S. Fish and Wildlife Service to establish its National

Eagle Repository, which collects dead birds and distributes them to Native Americans, who have a legal right to use them in ceremonies and who have signed on to a long waiting list.

However, some dispute that eagle feathers were ever used in ceremonies by certain groups that now employ them and believe the repository has created an artificial market that encourages people to kill eagles for profit. Also significant is the pow-wow circuit; some Aboriginal dancers add eagle feathers to their costumes to increase their chances of winning cash prizes. These dancers, too, may come from groups that did not use eagle feathers historically but may have adopted them as part of an evolving "pan-Indian" style. When the arrests were publicized, many were outraged at the killings. Online responses to a *Victoria Times-Colonist* report demanded harsher penalties, attacked Natives for using "cultural excuses" to kill wildlife and used the issue to attack Natives as parasites on Canadian taxpayers. Such objections overlook the fact that many Aboriginals regard eagle feathers with reverence and say they would not purchase them, that the Tseil-Watuth and Squamish First Nations assisted police in the investigation, that the market for eagle feathers also includes an international trade in Native artifacts and, possibly, pow-wows organized in Germany, Poland and Russia by European "Indianists" who emulate Indigenous cultures. Different styles of animal exploitation provide convenient channels for racist discourse: methods of exploitation practised by dominant groups are considered acceptable and normal while practices of subordinate groups are deemed illegitimate, cruel and inhuman. Regulation of animal exploitation is one means of group identity formation and legitimacy and of reinforcing hegemony. Because eagle feathers are unimportant among dominant groups, killing eagles to obtain them is considered unnecessary and wasteful, primitive and superstitious. However, killing other birds for other purposes, such as for food or for down pillows or coats, is considered reasonable and acceptable.

Assuming that not all (if any) commentators were vegan animal rights activists, one may pause to consider the outrage over eagle killings and to question why similar outrage was not directed at the slaughter of millions of other birds such as chickens, turkeys and ducks. Some argue that chickens, for example, are "raised to be eaten," as if this is a justification rather than mere statement of fact. Indeed, one might argue that this same fact makes the slaughter of chickens more deplorable, since the eagles at least had some opportunity to live a natural life before being killed, while chickens endure only frustration, anxiety and pain before they are slaughtered. Of course, eagles, like other predators, are socially constructed as majestic or noble birds, symbols of freedom, pride and power, and killing them is seen as a transgression of human aspirations. Yet the failure to regard chickens as worthy of any such respect reveals a lack of knowledge about their capabilities and individual qualities, as well as our habit of denigrating those we exploit as unworthy of compassion or consideration. This is a consistent phenomenon in the oppression of subordinate groups, who are "dehumanized" and depicted as "animal-like" in racist propaganda. Unsurprisingly, chickens, who may be the most-exploited of all animals, given the scale of the poultry industry, are among the animals we treat with the utmost contempt, hating them as we devour their flesh.

Historically, many types of animal abuse were practised in Canada, but we now recognize these practices as outdated and cruel. Defending them on the basis of tradition is no defence at all, merely an acknowledgement that these activities existed in the past. Sexism and slavery, in fact virtually all forms of cruelty and oppression, have been defended on the grounds of tradition, but that does not mean these practices have any moral justification and that there is any reason to continue them.

3. KILLING ANIMALS FOR FOOD

The Most Fundamental Form of Exploitation

The worst forms of animal exploitation and abuse, simply in terms of numbers, occur in production of food. No one knows how many animals are killed for food in Canada. Agriculture and Agri-Food Canada does not compile a total, complaining that provincial agriculture ministries cannot provide basic statistical data, although they do count some types of animals (or "commodities" as the government calls them, in keeping with the logic of capitalism) killed in federally inspected slaughterhouses. The Canadian Coalition for Farm Animals, using U.N. Food and Agriculture (FAO) statistics (which excludes certain species), estimates over 696 million animals are killed for food annually in Canada.

Generally, Canadians are ignorant about the nature of those animals. They are not recognized as individual sentient beings with interests but, as with the government's classification of them as commodities, considered things existing only for human purposes. Meat-eaters defend killing and consuming animals as personal choice, ignoring the fact that animals would make a personal choice not to be murdered. Using flawed reasoning, some argue that, because animals are "bred for" slaughter, slaughtering them is acceptable. Examining treatment of birds such as chickens and turkeys, it is difficult not to think that our dismissal of their interests has veered into active hatred. Comparing the suffering of animals we exploit is difficult, but, in terms of numbers and cruelties we force them to endure, chickens are among the most abused. Although anatomical and physiological evidence shows no major differences between birds and mammals in capacity to feel pain, we deny birds even minor moral considerations occasionally given to "higher" mammals. Subjecting them to lives of constant frustration and pain and ignorant of their actual abilities and behaviour, we denigrate chickens and turkeys as symbols of cowardice and stupidity, deserving of whatever cruelties we inflict on them. Butcher shops, restaurants and grocery chains depict them as enthusiastic victims who cannot imagine a more joyous fate than to be killed and consumed by us. Mythologies of oppression promote the idea that victims are not only suited for, but happy with, their exploitation: just as women enjoy being raped, animals want to be eaten. Euphemisms and images distance us from realities of meat-eating. Both animals and women are objectified, fragmented and consumed. Again, treatment of animals becomes a powerful metaphor for human oppression, as women complain of being treated "like pieces of meat." In the case of animals, consumption is more consistently literal, although some serial killers of women also eat their human victims. Meat is associated with masculine power and strength; eating it mirrors and represents patriarchal values (Adams 2000).

Our language makes the fate of animals their intrinsic purpose, excluding the possibility of their individual personhood and independent interests. Categorizing animals by functions we assign them, we designate some "food animals," normalizing practices of killing them and consuming their flesh. Most "food animals" are raised in factory farms, in conditions designed to maximize profits. No reason exists to romanticize small farms as paradises for animals, but factory farms turn their lives into nightmares. Factory farms are corporate-designed mechanisms to provide the cheap meat that industries train consumers to desire. Producing animals "humanely" (and one wonders how it is "humane" to raise animals to kill them) would put the price of their flesh out of reach for most consumers. In systems that consider animals mere commodities, units of production, suffering is inherent: humane farming is a myth. Laws concerning treatment of animals in farming practices are practically non-existent in Canada. Regulations that do exist are not meant to protect animals but rather regulate products made from their bodies, although even human health takes second place to industry's needs. Governments consider animal welfare a low priority and defer to animal-exploitation industries, allowing them to set their own standards and to police themselves through voluntary adherence to recommended codes of practice they design. These are accepted by the courts as establishing acceptable standards, meaning the most atrocious cruelties are condoned as standard operating procedure. While numerous references to "humane" treatment and "unnecessary suffering" exist in Canadian legislation concerning factory farms, they are undermined by the general assumption that some degree of suffering and pain is "necessary" and acceptable (Bisgould, King and Stoppard 2001). Nearly everyone accepts that inflicting "unnecessary" suffering on animals is wrong. While we may disagree on what constitutes necessity, it is clearly wrong to cause suffering and death to animals simply to satisfy our desires for "pleasure, amusement, or convenience" (Francione 2008). Yet, this constitutes the basis of most uses of animals. People justify the pain, suffering and death they impose on animals simply because they enjoy the taste of flesh in their mouths. Since we do not need to consume meat or other animal products to live a healthy life, no absolute necessity is involved.

Dangers to Human Health

Although corporations advertise animal products as necessary for health, research shows consumption is actually unhealthy, increasing risks of cancer, heart attack, stroke, diabetes and obesity, while diets free of animal products are healthiest (Campbell and Campbell 2006; Robbins 2001). Additional dangers include contamination by deadly bacteria such as E. coli, salmonella and listeria. Listeriosis killed at least twenty-two Canadians in 2008 after an outbreak at Maple Leaf Foods, whose president Michael McCain disparaged complaints as "tummy ache stuff" before agreeing to a $27 million settlement; rather than critically analyzing animal exploitation, media praised McCain's public relations skills and Maple Leaf's market recovery. Others also found the poisonings hilarious. During the investigation, federal Agriculture Minister Gerry Ritz quipped about "death by a thousand… cold cuts." After his jokes about listeria at the 2009 Couchiching conference in Orillia were broadcast on YouTube, Rory McAlpine, Maple Leaf vice-president and former deputy-minister of agriculture for B.C., was forced to apologize although he did not retract his notion that "accountability of the consumer" was necessary for food safety. A 2003 Toronto Public Health inspection found almost a third of city butcher shops had "significant" or "crucial" infractions (Cribb 2003). In the same year, licences were suspended for Aylmer Meat Packers for processing animals who died before reaching the slaughterhouse, and for Wallace Beef, a private contractor using convict labour at Pittsburgh Institution in Kingston, after allegations of "questionable practices" (CTV News 2003). After Canada's first report of "mad cow" disease (bovine spongiform encephalopathy, BSE) in 2003, a dozen cases had been found by 2008, and the Canadian Food Inspection Agency (CFIA) stated that it expected to find "a small number" more over the coming decade. Although BSE-infected meat has killed at least 150 people, mainly in Britain, the Canadian government is dedicated to protecting the beef industry and downplays the risks. In addition to directly endangering human health through consumption, animal agriculture does so indirectly as a major factor in perpetuating global poverty and degradation of our environment.

Industry Propaganda: Animal Welfare

Using "unnecessary suffering" as a standard effectively exempts "farm animals" from legal protection and concern about cruelty, because industries defend abuses as generally accepted practices. The existence of these industries and their use of animals remains accepted as legitimate "common sense." Although every year hundreds of millions of animals are subjected to hideous cruelty and abuse before they are killed, prosecutions for welfare violations are rare. Canadian law disregards farmed animals' interests almost entirely. The property status of animals means their interests will always be subordinated to those of their owners, and "humane treatment" will always be determined by our desire to exploit them efficiently. Animals endure an existence full of pain and deprivation, considered commodities in a system designed for profit and extraction of the maximum amount of flesh, eggs and milk at the lowest possible cost; financial interests of producers and consumers outweigh consideration of animals' interests and the weakness or absence of laws reinforces belief that animals' lives lack intrinsic value, that their pain does not matter and that we have no ethical obligations to them (Francione 1995). It is simply assumed that owners will avoid damaging their animal property in order to maintain its market value, inflicting only that suffering required for profit, which assumes that some degree of suffering is legitimized by such profiteering. As Francione argues, animal welfare laws are of limited value since they accept this and, rather than rejecting the use of animals in the first place, focus on modifying treatment. Bisgould, King and Stoppard (2001: 61–62) conclude:

> Canadian laws, despite paying lipservice to the societal expectation that we treat animals "humanely," actually regard animals as nothing more than production machines. Both on the federal and provincial levels, they facilitate the infliction of the most profound privation and suffering on hundreds of millions of individual animals on an annual basis.

Factory Farming: Chickens

Factory farms confine huge numbers of animals, keeping many indoors for their entire existence. They are crowded together, often without space to turn around or take more than a single step, let alone exercise normal behaviours. Mechanized production enables a few people to process thousands of animals. Poultry operations using laying hens to produce eggs confine birds in battery cages, with little room to move. About 98 percent of Canada's tens of millions of egg-producing hens are kept in small wire boxes for most of their lives. Cages measuring 16 in. x 18 in. and holding several birds are stacked in long rows in darkened sheds and excrement falls from the uppermost cages onto birds below. Normally, chickens engage in nesting, perching, scratching the ground and dust-bathing but confinement renders these behaviours impossible, thwarting their natural instincts. Hens are turned into machines, artificially induced to produce as many eggs as possible, weakening their bodies. They naturally lay eggs in privacy and under shelter and being to be forced to do so on the inclined wire-mesh floor while fully-exposed frustrates them; many retain their eggs for as long as possible, creating more stress. Barely able to move, they cannot exercise, and constant egg-production drains calcium; osteoporosis is widespread, rendering their bones fragile and easily broken.

The European Union adopted plans to phase out battery cages by 2012, and major food stores in Britain stopped selling eggs from battery caged hens. In November 2008, Californians voted to accept Proposition 2 (the *Prevention of Farm Animal Cruelty Act*), which takes effect in January 2015 and bans battery cages, as well as gestation crates for breeding sows and crates for veal calves. Prior to that, across North America, universities and colleges adopted cage-free policies, and in B.C., the cities of Richmond, Vancouver and Whistler announced that municipal cafeterias would only sell eggs from cage-free birds. Some Canadian producers recognized a niche market supplying consumers willing to pay higher prices for "specialty" eggs but we may question if this represents much improvement for animals. Welfarists hailed this as progress, but an animal rights approach rejects the idea of using animal at all, no matter how "humanely" they are treated.

Fewer than 3 percent of eggs sold in Canada are cage-free and the classification system is misleading. Eggs sold as "free range" are produced by chickens who have some ability to move indoors and outdoors but outdoor access is seasonal; "free run" means chickens are kept indoors but may have some access to nesting-boxes; "organic" means they receive organic grain. Canada has no real standards for what constitutes "free range" in terms of how much space birds have, the area in which they may move, the number of birds in the area, the duration of time they spend outdoors and so on. "Access" to the outdoors may be through a single entry-point and in the same overcrowded conditions this means only a few birds ever reach it. To the extent that such measures reduce suffering of some animals, they are improvements but, overall, "free range" and "cage free" classifications reflect only minor modifications that allow producers to charge higher prices and depict themselves as concerned with animal welfare while allowing consumers to feel more virtuous about consuming animal products. A more effective strategy for those concerned about suffering of birds, and other animals, is through vegan education (Francione 2007).

After less than two years, laying hens are considered "spent," meaning their bodies are too exhausted to produce eggs. Most are "spent" after one year. These weakened, fragile birds are pulled from their cages, suffering broken bones in the process, and sent to slaughterhouses that turn them into soup or pies, food for other animals or compost. Since birds bred for egg-production are thinner than those bred for meat, these chicks are worth little; they are ground up alive as feed for other animals, using high-speed macerators, similar to kitchen-sink garborators. Effective inspection is unlikely, and with no regulations governing what constitutes "high speed," some birds are ground up bit by bit. Because they are of little economic value, few processing-plants want them, so they may be trucked thousands of kilometres, suffering brutal treatment, temperature extremes, overcrowding, stress and lack of food and water. Since disposing of "spent" birds is a cost for producers, they prefer disposing of birds on-site, by the cheapest method: gassing, electrocution, beating them to death or bulldozing them into pits while still alive. Unwanted male chicks are also disposed of by the cheapest methods.

In 2005, Alberta Egg Producers (AEP) enthused about new killing technology, the modified atmosphere chamber, developed by Alberta Agriculture and Rural Development (AARD). This allows producers to dump 650 birds at a time into a huge bin and, using carbon dioxide, kill 30,000 per eight-hour-shift. AEP's Susan Gal beamed about "tremendous advantages for our industry," and John Church, AARD's animal welfare expert, pronounced it a humane way for Alberta's 170 registered egg farms to kill 1.6 million spent hens every year. However, University of Bristol poultry expert Dr. Mohan Raj says carbon dioxide causes birds to suffocate slowly, enduring great suffering (United Poultry Concerns 2005). Again, industry's goals of cost-cutting efficiency define "humane" treatment.

"Broiler" chickens raised for meat are held in buildings containing tens of thousands of birds. Genetic manipulation has transformed them into grotesque giants whose skeletons and cardiopulmonary systems cannot support their weight; many are crippled or die weeks after birth, and survivors develop cancers and other diseases. Although they may have space to move when young, it is reduced as they all grow, and as they approach the end of their artificially shortened lives (about seven weeks), they too are traumatized by overcrowding. Birds forced into close proximity, without room to roam freely, suffer stress and frustration, expressed in aggression towards others. Laying hens and broiler chickens alike inhabit a toxic atmosphere created by built-up waste excreted by huge numbers of animals in confined spaces. Broiler chickens suffer hock burns and blindness from wading through ammonia-saturated waste. Caged hens also endure ammonia burns, as many suffer severe feather loss from rubbing against the wire and exposing their sensitive skin to the toxic atmosphere.

To prevent tightly confined, frustrated animals from injuring each other before humans kill them, they are mutilated: some are castrated, de-horned and debeaked, others have their teeth cut and tails chopped off. Industry and government representatives use euphemisms such as "beak trimming" to depict mutilations as benign practices, similar to trimming one's fingernails. In reality, these procedures are extremely painful. In debeaking, up to two-thirds of a bird's beak is hacked off to deal with abnormal aggression created by overcrowded conditions. Veterinarians note that the beak contains a very sensitive layer of soft tissue and that cutting this causes severe pain. A bird's beak is a complex sense organ used in manipulating food and drinking and in nesting and exploring. When this is seared off with a hot blade, the bird is left stressed and depressed with a painful stump and experiences phantom limb sensations similar to those described by human amputees.

Cruelty was exposed in 2005 by a University of Guelph student who filmed conditions at L.E.L. Farms, an industrial-style operation run by Lloyd Weber, a veterinarian and a member of the Dean's Veterinary Advisory Council at the university. Video on the Canadian Coalition for Farm Animals website shows tattered, neglected birds living in darkness, kept in filthy, fecal-caked wire cages, and a dead bird in the aisle. Poultry scientist Mohan Raj expressed shock that Canada permitted such "extreme cruelty to layer hens" (Baumel 2006). Weber defended his operation, saying he had broken no laws and met the industry's code of practice. This was true: disgusting conditions are typical for the industry, which sets its own standards and defines "humane" treatment in its own terms; the basic legitimacy of these industries goes unquestioned. In fact, Weber's operation was a showcase for training University of Guelph students (prompting questions about how bad conditions were elsewhere) but following advice from the Ontario Farm Animal Council, an industry lobby and public relations group, Weber stopped giving tours.

Factory Farming: Other Birds

Along with chickens, millions of other birds are slaughtered every year in Canada after enduring a similarly deformed existence in factory farms. For example, turkeys normally roam freely but profit-maximizing factory farms pen them by the thousands in poorly ventilated barns. Like other commodified "farm animals," they are selectively-bred for heaviness and natural reproductive behaviour is impeded by their huge size, so artificial insemination is the norm. The joints of these gigantic birds cannot support the weight they rapidly gain from high-nutrient food. Crowding these large birds into small spaces causes aggression. To prevent damage to their animate property, producers cut off the birds' beaks and snoods, without anaesthetics, and keep them in darkness. Birds develop ulcers on their feet and lameness from standing in wet litter and their own excrement, while the toxic air produces respiratory diseases. Although turkeys normally live ten years, producers consider them "mature" and ready-for-slaughter after twelve and before twenty-six weeks.

When producers consider birds "ready" for killing, they are roughly captured and often injured from being thrown onto trucks for transport to slaughter. They can be transported for thirty-six hours without food or water. At the slaughterhouse, they are hung upside down and, supposedly, stunned by an electric current while being passed through a trough of water before their throats are cut and they are defeathered in scalding water. Emphasis on speed and the fact that the birds are struggling for their lives mean some are neither stunned nor killed and go through the whole process alive and conscious. In fact, the electricity is not strong enough to fully stun the birds but is intended to paralyze them for easier handling, to facilitate defeathering and to improve tenderness of their flesh. Birds are kept alive through slaughter so their hearts will continue to beat and they will bleed out (Lee, Hargus, Webb, Rickansrud and Hagberg 1979).

Such obvious cruelty prompts demands for reform and abolition but the food industry, unconcerned about animal welfare despite claims to the contrary, resists. For example, PETA waged its five-year Kentucky Fried Cruelty campaign against Priszm Income Fund, owner of KFC [Kentucky Fried Chicken]-Canada, Pizza Hut and Taco Bell. This involved 12,000 protests, including one at a Toronto

Blue Jays baseball game at which the Jumbotron screen displayed the message: "[Priszm chief executive] John Bitove and KFC Cripple Chickens." In June 2008, reeling from huge market value losses as many of its stores closed, KFC-Canada agreed to buy chickens from suppliers that used controlled-atmosphere killing, rendering birds unconscious with a mixture of argon, nitrogen and carbon dioxide. Gassing birds will not end suffering: demand for speed means birds may not remain in gas chambers long enough to be rendered unconscious, and because of the huge numbers processed in industrial slaughterhouses, some will regain consciousness before being killed. Again, we see that reforms often have little effect.

Foie Gras

Many birds suffer additional abuse in Canada's foie gras industry. Like the fur industry, foie gras production invests certain animal commodities with a supplemented symbolic value based on extra suffering. Marketed as a delicacy for elite consumers, foie gras ("fatty liver") is produced in animals suffering a disease: hepatic steatosis. A similar disease occurs in livers of humans who are alcoholics or suffer from obesity. Moulard ducks (produced by breeding male muscovy ducks with female pekin ducks) are commonly used to produce foie gras. As in other factory farms, they spend most of their lives confined in small wire cages, which prevent natural behaviour. They are force-fed with much more food than they would normally ingest, creating diseased and enlarged livers. Industrial production forces a tube down the bird's throat several times daily and feed is pumped in. Sometimes the tube punctures the bird's throat or ruptures internal organs, causing the animal to bleed to death. Many become too ill to stand after being put into production. Some aspirate food into their lungs and suffocate or choke to death. Swollen livers fail to perform properly in clearing toxins from the blood and impair the birds' ability to breathe and walk. Producers say ducks experience no discomfort from having metal tubes shoved down their throats and being force-fed. However, the European Union's Scientific Committee on Animal Health and Animal Welfare stated in 1998 that, in fact, ducks have a gag reflex similar to humans and the ducks find the experience distressing and easily can be injured, suffering tears in the trachea or esophagus. The Committee recommended prohibiting production, importation, distribution and sale of foie gras. In addition to animal suffering, the *Sunday Times* (June 17, 2007) reported that consuming foie gras may cause diseases such as Alzheimer's, type 2 diabetes and rheumatoid arthritis.

The United Nations Food and Agriculture Organization (FAO) and the World Society for the Protection of Animals (WSPA) expressed serious concerns about welfare violations related to foie gras and oppose its production, as do prominent veterinarians, including Dr. Ian Duncan, poultry welfare expert and professor in applied ethology at the University of Guelph. In 2007, the Humane Society of the United States, Farm Sanctuary, Animal Legal Defense Fund and the NYU Student Animal Legal Defense Fund legally petitioned the U.S. Department of Agriculture's Food Safety and Inspection Service to declare foie gras a diseased product unfit for human consumption. Austria, the Czech Republic, Denmark, Finland, Germany, Israel, Italy, Luxembourg, Norway, Poland and Turkey banned foie gras sales although France, world's largest producer, ignores international criticism, and in 2005, actually passed a law declaring foie gras part of its national heritage. The city of Chicago banned sale and production of foie gras although this was reversed under pressure from the restaurant industry. California announced a ban to take effect by 2012. Pope Benedict XVI denounced force-feeding birds as a violation of biblical principles, Prince Charles removed foie gras from the menu at his royal residences and actor Sir Roger Moore, known for his role as secret agent James Bond, stopped eating foie gras when he learned how it is produced and narrated a video for PETA opposing the industry. Although most food stores in Britain dropped the product, one target of Moore's campaign was Selfridges, owned by Canadian billionaire Galen Weston. Moore sent a letter to Weston, along with a video depicting cruelties involved in force-feeding but Selfriges refused to remove its "delicacy."

Much of the world rejects such obvious cruelty, even while endorsing other forms, but even this small step in moral progress is yet to be made in Canada. Quebec is one of the world's biggest foe gras producers. In 2007, Global Action Network released under-cover video taken at Quebec's largest producer, Elevages Perigord (a subsidiary of French corporation Excel Development), in St. Louis de Gonzague, southwest of Montreal. After having their beaks and toes cut off, ducks are force-fed with funnels rammed down their throats to enlarge their livers to ten times their normal size. Evidently, Perigord workers found the birds' suffering insufficient: they were shown kicking ducks, killing them by slamming them against a post, and ripping heads off animals. Andrew Plumbly, of Global Action Network, told CTV News: "All the females end up in the garbage where they just suffocate to death. It's because they produce smaller livers." The company responded by suspending one employee while denying that cruelty is involved. As Legault (2007) noted, the Quebec government's own Societe generale de financement provides 43 percent of Perigord's financing and "foie gras is a lucrative, govern-ment backed business. Chances are slim that Agriculture Canada and Quebec's Ministry of Agriculture will ever step up their own rules and supervision."

Global Action Network (2007) obtained video at another pro-ducer, Quebec Aux Champs d'Élisé, in Marieville, showing: "em-ployees slamming live ducks into the floor, grabbing ducks by their necks and throwing them through the air and force feeding ducks to the point where they vomited food stained bright red with blood from their damaged throats. One employee, a fifteen-year-old boy, was documented 'testing' his new hunting knife on a live duck by slowly cutting its throat." Animal advocacy group Liberation BC campaigned against Vancouver restaurants selling foie gras and complained to the Better Business Bureau against one, Le Gavroche, that advertised "humanely produced" foie gras that was actually from

Aux Champs d'Elise, where cruelty was exposed by Global Action Network.

Canadian grocery chains such as Loblaws, Dominion and Sobeys sell foie gras, and expensive restaurants promote it as a luxury for affluent diners unconcerned with animal suffering, including those claiming to be socially progressive: the *Toronto Star* (Mills 2005) described New Democratic Party (NDP) leader Jack Layton smearing foie gras on his toast at a Toronto restaurant. (The swipe at Layton's contradictory ethics was in terms of class, not animal rights, since the *Star* promotes animal products daily, through its food, lifestyle and restaurant columns, as well as in more obvious advertising.) Celebrity chefs and food writers tout foie gras, denouncing those who oppose cruelty as fanatics and extremists. Demonstrating lack of compassion for animals as well as callous disregard for humans victimized by actual terrorism, Anthony Bourdain (2001: 70), who opposed banning foie gras, called vegetarians "the worst kind of terrorists" and complained:

> Vegetarians, and their Hezbollah-like splinter faction, the vegans, are a persistent irritant to any chef worth a damn. To me, life without veal stock, pork fat, sausage, organ meat, demi-glace, or even stinky cheese is a life not worth living. Vegetarians are the enemy of everything good and decent in the human spirit, and an affront to all I stand for, the pure enjoyment of food.

Similarly, the chef at a London restaurant deploys typical arguments:

> I just wonder what the world would be like if those people put all that time, energy and money into helping the human suffering in this world rather than panicking about the mindset of a French goose that is going to be killed for meat in a matter of weeks. (Mallan 2008)

Evidently, since the goose will be killed, inflicting additional suffering is unproblematic; one wonders "what the world would be like" if the chef not only put his own energy into "helping the human suffering" but stopped promoting animal abuse to satisfy wealthy peoples' cruel tastes. Of course, it is "better" to kill birds after weeks of agonizing confinement without subjecting them to additional tortures of force-feeding, but campaigns to end foie gras production should be part of a broader struggle to end all forms of animal exploitation, not simply to reform some aspects and make them appear more humane.

Factory Farming: Pigs

Other animals are killed in Canada's "red meat industry": in 2007 this included 116,000 elk and deer, 220,000 bison, 879,000 sheep and lambs, 14.2 million cattle and 14.9 million hogs, raised on Canadian farms, often in appalling conditions. Pigs on factory farms spend most, if not all, of their lives in crates. Industry and government representatives say this is for their protection, since overcrowding provokes fighting. Millions of these highly intelligent animals are kept in two by seven foot cages, on cement floors, behind iron bars, allowed to move only one step forward or backward. Pigs are confined in these crates for their entire lives, then killed. Females are artificially inseminated and moved to gestation or farrowing crates that provide just enough room for the mother and babies. After ten to twenty-one days, they are returned to their regular stalls, which prevent normal activities and create lives of agony and frustration. Muscles atrophy and bones and joints weaken, making it difficult to support their artificially increased weight. Many become crippled and suffer infections. Blocked from walking, foraging, rooting or even moving normally, hogs become depressed and lethargic, engaging in stereotypic behaviour or withdrawing into themselves. Owners find it easier to raise pigs in crates, defending their cruelty with claims that pigs are aggressive and must be kept separated. Their solution is to stop interaction entirely and imprison hogs individually in cages, a solution denounced by most welfare specialists, even those unopposed to using animals in industrial farming. Furthermore, aggression is provoked by the anxiety of intensive confinement that prevents animals from establishing their own social orders. Animals trapped in these conditions are driven mad with fear and frustration and are more vulnerable to illness. Gestation crates were banned in Britain in 1999 and also are banned in Sweden. The European Union passed legislation to stop prolonged use of sow stalls by 2013. In 2002 Florida made these stalls illegal.

Even within the context of animal welfare — that strange philosophy of "improving" the lives of animals we imprison and slaughter without rejecting the very basis of that exploitation — the system of confining hogs in crates for their entire lives is recognized as an egregious violation of the industry's so-called five freedoms (from hunger and thirst; discomfort; pain, injury or disease; to express normal behaviour; from fear and distress).

Canada is a significant global exporter of pork, with billions in annual profits, controlled mainly by two corporations, Maple Leaf Foods and Olymel. Business boomed after 2000, especially in Manitoba. In 2007, Manitoba produced 9.4 million pigs, accounting for 31.5 percent of national production, surpassing Ontario and Quebec (each producing about 23 percent). Industry supporters called it an economic miracle for Manitoba, with growth unparalleled in North America and providing nearly half the province's cash receipts. The miracle was fuelled by a grain crisis due to termination of federal transportation subsidies (the Crow Rate), meaning farmers had to pay more to move crops to market; increased livestock production provided alternative ways to sell grain. With meat consumption growing globally, corporate agribusiness found a welcoming government in Manitoba. It provided over seven million dollars in subsidies and tax-breaks to Maple Leaf Foods to build its massive killing plant in Brandon and allowed the corporation to take over other slaughterhouses in Winnipeg. Corporations considered Manitoba cost-efficient in terms of government financial support, lax environmental enforcement and cheap land, feed, and labour. Maple Leaf demanded a seven-year agreement with the United Food and Commercial Workers and cut wages 40 percent before opening its Brandon slaughterhouse.

Things were less miraculous for the hogs, who were processed at dizzying speed. Maple Leaf Foods' Brandon slaughterhouse was killing 2.5 million per year and planned a double shift so they could kill 4.5 million per year (86,000 per week), while Springhill Farms in Neepawa killed about 80,000 per year.

Workers who kill and eviscerate animals face dangerous conditions, experiencing high rates of injury and respiratory diseases from dust and toxic air. Unsurprisingly, it was hard to find people to do these tasks, especially at Maple Leaf, where wages are among the lowest for all Canadian slaughterhouses. Maple Leaf began recruiting Mexicans and Salvadorans as temporary foreign workers, making them sign agreements preventing them from changing jobs when they discovered they could earn higher wages for killing animals elsewhere, such as at Springhill Farms.

Hogwatch Manitoba and the Waterkeeper Alliance warned that giant hog farms, which devastated North Carolina's environment, would do the same in Manitoba. North Carolina's hog factories contained millions of hogs and stored huge open lagoons of waste, typically in poor and predominantly black areas. When hurricanes hit in 2000, they released a flood of millions of gallons of untreated waste, along with carcasses of drowned animals, polluting vast areas. Manitobans worried about the potential for environmental disaster in their flood-prone province. As in North Carolina, Manitobans living near these huge factory farms experienced an unbearable stench that kept them prisoners in their now-devalued homes, unable to enjoy outdoor activities. By 2008, Manitoba's miraculous hog industry found itself in crisis due to falling hog prices, rising feed prices linked to subsidized ethanol production and a strong Canadian currency. In 2009, anxiety over the swine flu pandemic and changes in U.S. labelling laws weakened the hog industry further, as the federal government promised $75 million to help farmers leave the industry.

Factory Farming: Cows

Canada is a top exporter of cattle and beef, although Canadians like eating cows themselves, consuming 49.4 pounds per capita in 2001. Cows raised for beef may range in fields for part of their lives before confinement in feedlots, where they are fattened on an unnatural grain diet prior to transport to slaughter. Although less-painful methods exist to mark ownership, branding their flesh with a red-hot iron is still considered acceptable; government-run websites such as Alberta's Livestock Identification Services provide instructions on branding and castration by cutting off testicles with knives, crushing blood vessels with clamps or cutting blood supply to testicles with rubber rings, a procedure banned in some European countries. If conducted for amusement by individuals, such practices would be considered sadistic but when defined as necessary for profit, anything goes.

Dairy cows spend much of their lives chained in stalls, especially in winter. Artificially inseminated, kept constantly pregnant and filled with hormones and chemicals, they are transformed into milk-producing machines. Genetic modification and hormone use forces cows to produce much more milk than they normally would. One consequence is mastitis, inflammation of the udders, which is treated with antibiotics. Calves, byproducts of this milk-production process, are removed from their mothers, castrated and sent to the veal industry. In Ontario alone, up to 700 veal farms generate hundreds of millions of dollars by keeping baby cows isolated and penned, often in dark sheds.

The Canadian Agri-Food Research Council recommends allowing enough light for calves to see one another for eight hours a day, suggests that stalls for individually confined animals should "allow the calf to get up and lie down without difficulty" and says a stall width of "70 cm (27.5 in) untethered and 80 cm (31.5 in) tethered is generally accepted." The Council does not indicate how these standards came to be "generally accepted" or who determines this, but, clearly, industries basically set their own rules. The Ontario Veal Association (n.d.), which promotes consumption of calves' flesh, characterizes these conditions as a service to them, allowing individual feeding, disease prevention and a "safe, comfortable environment where they can get up, turn around and socialize with other animals." For animals tethered in individual stalls, "socialization" is limited to only seeing other prisoners. Characterizing death row as a "safe" environment is Orwellian obfuscation, industry propaganda for "humane" meat. Meat, egg and dairy industries are major advertisers so media consent is guaranteed, with dissenting voices muted. Nevertheless, reporters sometimes receive bribes for enthusiastic support; for example, by providing "a six-course veal luncheon for the media," the Ontario Veal Association received laudatory coverage in the *Toronto Star* (Bain 2007), which praised "humane" production and succulent taste, while ignoring confinement, deprivation and mutilation and normalizing the premature death of sentient beings.

In transport to slaughterhouses, animals are crowded into trucks, exposed to extreme temperatures and denied food and water. Thousands die during transport but this is part of projected costs, and subsidiary industries deal with their corpses. Formerly, "downer" animals unable to walk were dragged off trucks by chains or ropes and processed with others. Following discovery of "mad cow disease" in Canadian cattle and closing of foreign markets, in 2005 the CFIA declared transporting non-ambulatory animals illegal. This was designed to protect sales, not a humane initiative. Ambulatory animals could still be transported to the nearest slaughterhouse even if plainly in great distress and at risk of becoming downers when suffering from exhaustion, dehydration, body temperature and heart rate above or below normal, nervous system disorders, open wounds, bleeding, exposed bones, blindness in both eyes or rectal prolapse (CFIA n.d.). Even as the whole industry was endangered and the health of humans who consumed diseased animals was threatened, the decision caused protests from producers who complained about losing immediate profits.

Because industrial slaughter "processes" large numbers of

animals as quickly as possible, many are not fully stunned and are skinned alive. Others are beaten to death. Inspections are announced in advance, and where inspectors are regularly on hand, they serve the interests of industry, not animals. Considering the intelligence, emotional capacities and physical and psychological characteristics of "food animals," factory farming obviously violates their essential needs. Despite intensive propaganda about "caring" about animals, industries confine them in systems designed to thwart every aspect of their normal behaviour before ending their lives prematurely.

Exotic Flesh

Canada produces many types of "exotic" flesh. Millions of bison inhabited the prairies in the nineteenth century, but hunting and transformation of their habitat into farmland nearly drove them to extinction; only about 1,000 remained at the beginning of the twentieth century. Now, producers and restaurants specializing in "game" meats promote bison as a natural or healthy food. From 2001 to 2006, the number of bison increased almost 35 percent and slaughter more than doubled, from 11,168 to 25,613 individuals, as did exports of their flesh. Bison are farmed mainly in the prairie provinces. Although not confined in overcrowded conditions that other "farm animals" endure, their lives are truncated. Bison live twenty-five years but are considered "ready" or "finished" at between twenty and thirty months, although market pricing determines the duration of their lives. When a market exists for smaller carcasses and brings higher prices, animals are killed earlier.

Other "novelty" meat is made from wild boar, goats and ducks but production declined after 2000. The Canadian government provided over a million dollars in grants and loans for ostrich, emu and rhea farmers, and at one point the industry was worth over $1 billion but consumption was less than anticipated; flesh of these animals is mainly sold in upscale restaurants. Rabbits, originally produced in Canada as raw material for hats, came to substitute for "traditional" meats after the Second World War. Although production is on a smaller scale than factory farming of other animals, rabbits endure similar conditions, packed into stacked-up rows of crowded cages, and suffer the same injuries, infections and cruelties in transport and slaughter as do other animals consigned to such grim fates. In 2006, the Canadian government recorded 600,000 rabbits slaughtered in inspected slaughterhouses but many more are slaughtered elsewhere and still others are raised for vivisection, where their agonies are further prolonged.

Opposing Exploitation

All these forms of exploitation are opposed by animal advocates who promote vegetarianism or veganism. While vegetarianism is not always linked to ethical concerns for animals, it is the basic diet for many people, especially in India, where most of the population is vegetarian. India's most famous exponent of vegetarianism, Mahatma Gandhi, linked vegetarianism with *ahimsa*, the practice of nonviolence, arguing that a vegetarian diet was conducive to living in accordance with principles of *ahimsa*. He was influenced to seriously readopt vegetarianism and to incorporate it into his political philosophy by Henry Salt's *Plea for Vegetarianism* (1886), which associated vegetarianism with animal rights. Contemporary activists share many concerns with Gandhi and Salt and consider veganism the basic expression of a civilized outlook, the foundation of a progressive engagement with the world.

Rather than taking an animal rights-based approach and rejecting the use of animals, Canadian welfare organizations pursue contradictory and limited campaigns to make agribusiness more "humane." Welfarist approaches criticize various cruelties, such as factory farming, but accept the basic premise that animals can be exploited for human ends. Failing to recognize contradictions between animal welfare and animal rights, between those who accept the exploitation of animals and those who do not, the group Friendly Manitoba (n.d.)

claims: "Whether conscientious meat eater, vegetarian, or vegan, we are united in the movement towards a food system that promotes socially responsible agriculture, healthy and safe food, and thriving rural communities." The Beyond Factory Farming Coalition (n.d.) promotes "socially responsible livestock production," while Canadians for Ethical Treatment of Food Animals (n.d.) works "towards the compassionate treatment of food animals, so that their lives may be free from pain and fear, followed by a humane death." The Canadian Coalition for Farm Animals opposes battery cages and sow stalls and promotes the welfare of animals raised for food. These groups do not challenge the foundations of animal exploitation but instead propose modifications to specific practices. Larger welfare groups like the International Fund for Animal Welfare and the World Society for the Protection of Animals do not even mention vegetarianism and give little attention to the plight of animals farmed for food, which is the most extensive form of animal exploitation. Factory farming systems were created to maximize profits, but industries are willing to make inexpensive reforms that may lessen suffering if they can still profit. For example, production of "humanely raised meat" or "cage-free eggs" supplies a niche market for affluent consumers willing to pay more to exploit animals "ethically." It is impossible to provide meat to all who wish to eat it through such a system; only elite consumers can afford it, but corporations recognize that this niche market will yield significant profits. The property status of animals, economics of production and basic moral problem that animal exploitation inevitably involves some degree of torture, make it not just difficult but impossible to make exploitation more "humane," rendering welfarism ineffective (Francione 2009). Such efforts are akin to seeking nicer forms of slavery and murder. Producing animals for food is a fundamental contradiction in Canadians' claims to abhor "unnecessary" suffering. Since shifting to an inexpensive, healthy diet without animal products is simple, moral progress requires that we seriously consider animals' interests and become vegan.

4. KILLING ANIMALS FOR FUN

Paradise for Killers

Canadian identity is linked with images of animals and the environment they inhabit. Originally seen as a supplier of fish and fur and, now, in tourist advertisements featuring moose, bears and whales, Canada is imagined as a vast wilderness, a sporting paradise full of animals to be hunted. Almost all this killing is done for entertainment. Although necessary for some humans in the past, it certainly is not feasible for the general human population as a means of survival. Subsistence hunters are rare today; even those who eat the animals they kill usually do so to supplement their diets rather than depending exclusively on hunting. Few Canadians make a living primarily by hunting. Service B.C. (2005: 10) estimated only "about 140 people worked as commercial hunters and trappers" in the province, some probably only part-time. Most hunters kill for sport, although this is misleading since the term indicates a voluntary pastime that provides recreation and pleasure (commercialization adds other motives). In the "sport" of hunting, only humans voluntarily participate and enjoy the process; animals are chased, terrified and killed. Hunters enjoy stalking animals and violently ending their lives, practices that should give pause even to those who do not accept that other animals have a right to life. Like other abusers, hunters claim to respect, even "love," animals they kill. Discourses of exploitation are remarkable for how consistently those who harm animals use the terminology of love. Farmers who sell animals to slaughterhouses, vivisectors who poison and torture, hunters who stalk and kill, all claim to love those they victimize. None of their actions correspond to what we normally consider expressions of love, and it is difficult to imagine what additional horrors could be inflicted upon animals if their tormentors were motivated by malice rather than the tender concern they claim to feel. Hunters believe they have a "right" to kill animals simply because they are not human. Like other animal exploiters, they assert ownership over their prey. Hunters consider animals their property, although it is unclear why their assertion takes precedence over that of others who may prefer photographing "their" animals, or simply leaving them alone.

Hunting for food is more expensive than purchasing meat in stores. Rather than being a subsistence activity, hunting is a profitable industry, providing a huge array of products and services to elite hunters who pay thousands of dollars to kill animals for entertainment. Many government departments depend on funding from sales of permits and licences and even aid the "sport" by artificially manipulating wildlife populations. Hunting ranches and lodges sell canned hunts, guaranteeing kills by keeping animals in a restricted area. Many lure animals with food so hunters can sit in one spot waiting for their victims to appear. Outfitters and guides offer packages to wealthy hunters, gearing price lists to species and size. So-called "ethical" hunters ostensibly scorn canned hunts, where animals are enclosed and cannot flee, and espouse "fair chase," where, supposedly, animals have opportunities to escape. This is not motivated by compassion for animals (otherwise hunters simply would abstain from hunting) but by desire to maximize pleasure in killing through making the process more challenging, a greater test of "skill." In fact, advanced technology gives hunters almost unlimited capacity to kill, eliminating any element of contest or risk, except from other hunters. While presenting this sordid violence as a spiritual quest, "ethical" hunters, too, degrade animals into commodities to be bought and sold.

Killing animals for sport has long been an expression of power. Hierarchical, patriarchal, militaristic and violent attitudes underlying hunting are the same ones that promote other forms of oppression. A society claiming to value compassion and wishing to foster it cannot endorse murder of animals for pleasure and sport. That many serial killers of humans first indulge their dark impulses by killing animals further confirms these as activities we should not encourage.

Lobbying for Killers

Sport hunting is an industry promoted by organizations like the Safari Club International (SCI), a wealthy, influential lobby group that opposes and undermines animal-protection laws so big-game hunters can kill animals (Hoyt 1995). In the U.S., the SCI attempts to weaken the *Endangered Species Act* so vulnerable species can be hunted and hunters can import their body parts as trophies. One tactic is to downgrade status, so species are merely "threatened" rather than "endangered" and, thus, can be killed. To advance its claims, the SCI commissions reports and submits them to governments. Even with species where only a few animals exist and where common sense indicates that every effort should be made to protect them, the SCI argues that killing them will have minimal impact on species survival. Portraying big-game hunting as an environmentally friendly activity that helps both animals and humans, the SCI persuaded the U.S. Congress to amend the *Marine Mammal Protection Act* to allow importation of polar bear trophies from Canada. At that time, U.S. and German hunters were paying $15,000 each to kill bears and the SCI said high prices equaled conservation. However, if bears are so lucrative, the Inuit will certainly use their full quota, whereas if they were hunted only for subsistence, that might not be the case (Hoyt 1995). At its 2008 meeting in Wyoming, the SCI discussed expanding its presence in Canada, "taking into account the vast abundance and diversity of Canadian wildlife Canada's strong hunting heritage and world-class conservation." Planners discussed establishing an SCI

Canada Foundation as a charitable front for the organization while engaging in hunting advocacy.

The SCI and its partners promote "sustainable use," regulated killing of managed animal populations, which are considered resources to be harvested like other crops. Organizations such as the International Union for Conservation of Nature (IUCN) and the World Wildlife Fund (WWF) promote this approach, advising that animals be "wisely used" at a rate that allows species to survive, even as individuals are killed for human purposes. These organizations say regulated consumption of animals will provide local human populations with economic incentives not to kill them all. However, history shows many species driven to extinction; desire for short-term profits leads humans to exploit animals as extensively as possible rather than selectively "harvesting" limited numbers.

Although purportedly based on ecological wisdom, neoliberal speciesist discourse of "sustainable use" considers animals only as resources to be managed for human benefit. Unless species "pay their way" through the sacrifice of individual animals, they have no right to exist. Only human desires count: animals' subjectivity and interests are excluded. In reality, sustainable use is simply a means to justify commercial killing of any species, even endangered ones, as long as humans profit financially.

In this Orwellian discourse, animals are killed so they can be conserved. Representing themselves as defenders of wildlife, conservationist groups actually defend the hunting industry. Rather than preserving lives because of intrinsic value, animals are conserved so that hunters have a steady supply to kill. This contradicts what most people understand by "conservation": preserving individual animals' lives and helping species to survive.

One of the SCI's partners is the Canadian Circumpolar Institute (CCI). Established at the University of Alberta in 1960 to promote research on Canada's North, it now promotes "sustainable use." The CCI considers wildlife a resource for humans to exploit and encourages sport hunting, not only in northern Canada but internationally.

The land-locked CCI houses the International Network for Whaling Research, directed by anthropologist Milton Freeman. Like Japan's euphemistic description of its commercial killing of whales, the CCI presents its pro-whaling stance as "research." In 1986 Freeman opposed a commercial whaling moratorium by the International Whaling Commission (IWC). A member of the World Council of Whalers, Freeman rejects any restriction on whaling, claiming that anti-whaling arguments are emotional, not scientific, and that they victimize whaling cultures. However, Freeman's own data was challenged, the IWC expressing concern about much lower numbers of whales. The CCI presents itself as a saviour of rural communities and wildlife as a resource for community "empowerment," and it promotes trophy hunting for profit. Wishing to improve conditions in impoverished Indigenous communities is commendable, but hunting proponents such as the CCI provide only one option. It regards animals only in instrumental terms, as objects and commodities, the property of those who pay to kill them. The CCI organizes conferences promoting messages acceptable to its pro-hunting funders, such as the SCI, the Safari Club North America and the Alberta Professional Outfitters Society, and presenting trophy hunting as essential to rural communities' "sustainability." Another funder, the Alberta Conservation Association (ACA), calls hunters and trappers "the key to conservation" and works with corporate partners, mainly oil companies and the paper giant Daishowa, subject of a 1991 international boycott for logging unceded territory claimed by the Lubicon Cree in northern Alberta. Corporations that destroy Aboriginal communities, extract their resources and pollute their environment support hunting and trapping as a cheap public relations strategy to show "concern" for Indigenous people.

The ACA gets $10 million annually from levies on provincial hunting and fishing licences, purchases land for hunting and conducts advertising campaigns such as its 2008 "Take Time for Tradition" push to emphasize "traditional values" associated with hunting and fishing and to encourage those who have given up hunting to resume killing animals. The association runs a $500,000 per year retention and recruitment program with its members, which include hunting and trapping associations and outfitters. Like hunting associations elsewhere, it recognizes that interest in hunting is waning. For example, Canadian Wildlife Services reported that waterfowl hunting dropped from 505,000 permit holders in 1970 to 134,910 in 2005. In the U.S., the 2006 National Survey of Fishing, Hunting and Wildlife-Associated Recreation said the number of hunters had fallen to 12.5 million, the lowest since 1970. In many European countries, the number of hunters has dropped by approximately half since the 1990s (Heberlein, Serup and Ericsson 2008: 444). Hunting groups attempt to reverse this trend by encouraging children to kill animals and by promoting hunting among women and disabled people. Federal and provincial government departments financially depend on hunting, fishing and trapping so they have direct interests in perpetuating these activities, despite the fact that public interest is declining as hunting becomes more expensive, attitudes towards animals become more advanced and killing animals for entertainment becomes less popular. As a result, governments introduced special children's programs. In 2000, the federal government declared the first week of September as Waterfowler Heritage Days, allowing people aged between twelve and seventeen to hunt prior to the regular hunting season, if accompanied by an adult, who is not allowed to carry or shoot a weapon.

In Alberta, where hunting licences fell from 162,573 in 1982–83 to 94,310 in 2005–06, Minister for Sustainable Resource Development Ted Morton, himself an avid hunter and fisherman, declared September 22 Hunting Day in 2007 as an effort to revive interest. In B.C., where hunting licence purchases dropped from 180,000 in 1981 to 85,000 in 2006, the Ministry of the Environment announced a plan in 2007 to increase hunters by 20,000 through targeting women and children. Recognizing that few who do not hunt when young take it up later, the government recruits children before they are old enough to recognize hunting as a primitive and violent pursuit. The government proposed lowering licence fees, extending the age limit for less-expensive junior licences to eighteen years and relaxing rules for new hunters, allowing them to hunt for a full season without taking a safety course if accompanied by a licensed hunter. Considering how many hunters shoot other hunters or bystanders while trying to kill animals, reducing safety requirements hardly seems wise.

The CCI and conservation groups such as the Canadian Wildlife Federation and provincial wildlife federations present themselves as defenders of wildlife, selling calendars and soliciting donations to "save animals," but rather than valuing animals' lives, these groups are part of the wildlife industry, which is based on killing animals for profit. If the CCI and other conservationist groups were really interested in the future of rural communities they would encourage ecotourism. Many more people enjoy visiting, watching and photographing wildlife than are interested in killing them for sport. The CCI and other conservationist groups ignore ecotourism and focus exclusively on killing animals, suggesting that it is not rural communities but the sport hunting industry that is their real concern.

Ideologists for Murder

The CCI academics romanticize hunting. For example, Lee Foote, in the University of Alberta's Renewable Resources Department, is hailed on pro-hunting websites for his *Heart of Darkness*-like murder fantasy, "The Irreducibility of Hunting." It first appeared in *Fair Chase*, a publication of the Boone and Crockett Club, which styles itself as a conservation organization but promotes killing competitions and scoring system for trophy hunters. Contrasting civilized behaviour to a "natural way of living," Foote says hunting expresses ancestral instincts underlying our civilized veneer and allows us to "move back in time." Acknowledging that sports provide similar excitement, Foote prefers hunting because it involves killing someone, the "absolute finality and gravity in deliberately stopping a heart." He is "purely happy" when killing because he experiences "pure escape from the socio-cultural material world" and contacts his primal brain's "dark and pure urges." Essentially, Foote just likes killing and seeks mystical justifications. No doubt, serial killers of humans express similar sentiments; the simple fact that one enjoys an activity does not legitimize it.

Another "wise use" proponent is Randall Eaton, whose website identifies him as a CCI research associate. Eaton writes pro-hunting stories for *Sports Illustrated*, *Outdoor Life* and *Bowhunter* and is a motivational speaker for hunting groups. Lecturing to the Ontario Federation of Anglers and Hunters, he suggested "hunting is good medicine for bad kids" and that delinquent boys will learn compassion by killing (Eaton n.d.,a). Like Foote, Eaton is ecstatic when killing, declaring himself "enraptured" when hunting, which he calls a "sacred path," "a religious ceremony" and "a holy communion, the original sacrificial rite" (n.d.,e). He, too, contacts "ancestral memory" when engaged in "Cro Magnon hunting rituals." He claims: "in a past life I was a shaman who killed another shaman when he (his spirit) was in the body of a deer" (Eaton n.d.,b). Calling hunting a sacred act and a male rite of passage, Eaton equates it with Native American vision quests, employing romanticized images of Indigenous people. Professing admiration for and emulation of Indigenous practices and attempts to clothe killing in spiritual camouflage are recent tactics in struggles to assert ownership over animals. In this case, Aboriginal people are stereotyped as hunters when in fact many Indigenous societies subsisted mainly on plants. Rita Laws (1994) says her own ancestors, the Choctaw farmers of Mississippi and Oklahoma, subsisted on a mainly vegetarian diet. Their daily food was a stew of corn, pumpkin and beans; their bread was made of acorns and corn, and small animals were eaten occasionally. Their houses were not made from animal skins but constructed of wood, cane, bark and mud, and their clothing was plant-based. All such practices are overlooked by focusing only on images of (male) Aboriginal hunters. When convenient, First Nations hunters are extolled as Noble Savage conservationists and, through magical transformations, used to defend sport hunting, just as the fur industry uses Indigenous people as marketing tools. However, in the nineteenth and through the mid-twentieth century, European big-game hunters and Canadian wildlife managers frequently depicted First Nations people as "un-sportsman-like," wasteful and indiscriminate killers of animals; those who killed for food were marginalized in favour of those who killed for trophies (Loo 2006).

Bizarrely equating killing with love, Eaton (n.d.,b) says during hunting "the instinctive or primal self merges with the spiritual. It is a vertical convergence of the subconscious to superconscious." He describes these vague processes in sexual/mystical terms: "Hunting is how we fall in love with nature. The basic instinct links up with the spiritual, and the result is that we become married to nature."

Eaton believes that "Just as females are biologically adapted to reproduce, males are adapted to hunt, kill and provide" (n.d.,b). Eaton (n.d.,c) calls killing a "fundamental instinct" in boys, one that initiates them into manhood, and explains: "A woman dare not interrupt this fragment of an age old rite, the oldest rite of them all, a sacred homage of the men to the wild animal" (n.d.,b). Inspired by Robert Bly's men's movement, with its emphasis on father-son bonding, Eaton (n.d.,d) claims:

> The hunt is as archetypal to males as birthing is to females. The hunt marries young men to wild animals and nature just as birthing bonds a young women [sic] to children and life. Men are adapted to take life to serve life. Hunting itself teaches universal virtues, and the taking of life opens hearts and engenders respect and responsibility.

Quoting Bly's claims that boys must indulge their instinct to hunt and live mythologically through the past in order to self-actualize, Eaton (n.d.,e) overlays these mystical notions with essentialist gender roles: "Hunting and killing are as fundamental to adult male evolution as birthing and infant care have been to women." Equating sex with killing, he suggests: "In hunting, the counterpart to falling in love is the death of the animal" (n.d.,e). Others are even more explicit in linking killing with sexual pleasure. For example, Dudley Young describes an "erotic connection" between hunter and prey and the hunter's "sexual ecstasy" at killing (quoted in Kheel 1996: 38).

As do innumerable pro-hunting websites, Eaton quotes assertions by Spanish philosopher Jose Ortega y Gasset. All quote the same muddled passage as if it contained insight:

> To the sportsman the death of the game is not what interests him; that is not his purpose. What interests him is everything that he had to do to achieve that death — that is, the hunt. Therefore what was before only a means to an end is now an end in itself. Death is essential because without it there is no authentic hunting: the killing of the animal is the natural end of the hunt and that goal of hunting itself, not of the hunter. The hunter seeks this death because it is no less than the sign of reality for the whole hunting process. To sum up, one does not hunt in order to kill; on the contrary, one kills in order to have hunted. (Ortega y Gasset 1985: 96–97)

Perhaps worried that their careers are insufficiently manly, other academics endorse recreational exploitation of animals to reinforce male camaraderie. For example, University of Toronto philosophy professor Mark Kingwell, interviewed for *Outdoor Canada*, describes fishing trips as male bonding exercises. The *National Post* described Alberta Minister for Sustainable Resource Development Ted Morton's hunting trips with University of Calgary neoconservative ideologues, Tom Flanagan, David Bercuson, Barry Cooper and Rainer Knopff, as opportunities to share ideas about abolishing welfare, assimilating Indians and attacking liberals, multiculturalists and feminists (Mitchinson 2000).

Although Eaton uses New Age rhetoric to promote hunting

as part of the Men's Movement, hunting associations are more traditionally sexist. For example, when "new hunter Roma Czech" wanted to improve her shooting skills and applied for membership in "her local anglers and hunters club in southern Ontario," she was told women could not join, although she was "welcome to join the women's auxiliary, where she could help cook the wild game dinner once a month. And one more thing: she couldn't leave the kitchen to eat with the men" (Schiedel 2001).

Facing declining numbers, hunting clubs must modify sexist policies; although most hunters are men, clubs are recruiting new hunters by encouraging women to kill animals. Alberta's Hunting for Tomorrow Foundation operates women's programs, the Ontario Federation of Anglers and Hunters (OFAH) runs Women's Outdoor Weekends, and New Brunswick's Department of Natural Resources offers the Becoming an Outdoorswoman course, created in the U.S. Another U.S. import is the Women in the Outdoors program, developed by the National Wild Turkey Federation, which tries to create new images of women in media. Canadians can watch cable television sports channels that feature women in programs, such as B.C.'s "Fishing with Shelley and Courtney" and "Outdoor Quest," featuring "The Outdoor Chicks" from Alberta. The Saskatchewan Wildlife Federation recently elected its first female president, Joyce Lorenz. Pro-hunting women influence government policies, exemplified by outfitter Sandy Dickson, chair of Ontario's Fish and Wildlife Advisory Board, who advises the province's Minister of Natural Resources. In 2008, women hunters were inspired by Sarah Palin's campaign for U.S. vice-president, which emphasized her moose-hunter qualifications; other candidates, including Hilary Clinton, scrambled to demonstrate their own accomplishments in killing animals, using this to prove they were Ordinary Janes with dominionist family values.

Although ecofeminists show links between oppression of animals and of women (Kheel 2008), evidently, some women consider it empowering to kill animals. Most women hunters are recruited by their husbands (male hunters are usually indoctrinated by fathers), begin hunting at a later age, seldom hunt without males and are less committed (Heberlein, Serup and Ericsson 2008: 445–51). Efforts to manipulate legislation may distort actual numbers: a study of Alberta licensing found that approximately one-third of female hunters applied for a permit to increase chances of a male hunter in the household getting a permit, suggesting that female participation might decline if changes occurred in the licensing system (McFarlane, Watson and Boxall 2003).

Addressing the hunting crisis but apparently misinformed about human evolution, the Michigan Hunter Recruitment and Retention Work Group (2006: 1) claims to represent "a tradition that has been in existence for more than 5 million years" and estimates that hunters contribute $30 billion per year to the U.S. economy and $490 million in Michigan itself in 2001; troubled by declining participation, the group suggests sacrificing glorification of male prowess to recruit women and children. The cover shows a camouflage-clad mother and daughter sharing joys of killing and the report contains several photographs of children being instructed in weapons training. The group presents squalid practices of killing animals for entertainment as noble and spiritual activities, citing standard ideologues, starting with Randall Eaton:

> We hunt because we love it…. Among nature pursuits, hunting and fishing connect us most profoundly with animals and nature…. When we hunt we experience extreme alertness to the point of an altered state of consciousness. (Michigan Hunter Recruitment and Retention Work Group 2006: 3)

Ortega y Gasset follows:

> It is a vacation from the human condition… that submerges man deliberately into something of a religious rite and emotion in which homage is paid to what is divine, transcendent,

in the laws of nature. (Michigan Hunter Recruitment and Retention Work Group 2006: 5)

Lee Foote is next:

> Hunting continues to renew us, give us humbling mortality insights, and provide hope for our next role escape. There are so very few things in our lives that yield these most precious of gifts: renewal, humility, insight, and hope. We must treat hunting with the same reverence we hold for our religions, our children, and the world's greatest works of art. (Michigan Hunter Recruitment and Retention Work Group 2006: 6)

None of these ideologues explain why such profound insights and emotions could not be obtained through saving the life of an animal through adoption or volunteering at a sanctuary.

World Conservation Trust

Eaton's mystical maunderings are considered serious philosophy and reproduced on the website of the World Conservation Trust (WCT), an anti-animal rights group that promotes all commercial exploitation of animals as "sustainable use." The WCT website links to groups such as Canada's National Firearms Association, Friends of Fur, the pro-whaling High North Alliance and Asian Wildlife Consultancy, which advises on wildlife management for zoos. The WCT is run by Eugene Lapointe, who grew up hunting in Quebec before obtaining a law degree from Laval University and becoming secretary-general of the Convention on International Trade in Endangered Species (CITES). Lapointe was fired from CITES in 1989 after being exposed for campaigning against a ban on the ivory trade, although he later received a settlement for "arbitrary" dismissal.

Lapointe promotes hunting, fishing, whaling, use of fur and all forms of commercial exploitation of animals as conservation tactics.

However, Richard Leakey, head of Kenya's Wildlife Service says: "Trade has been the foremost factor in the decimation of scores of species ranging from tigers to cod" (Vidal 2004). Opposing South Africa's efforts to resume the ivory trade, Leakey says even limited resumption would endanger wildlife, encourage poaching and have insignificant effects on human poverty. While "sustainable use" arguments may sound rational, Leakey notes the major difference between ecological and economic sustainability and that economic priorities are always given precedence.

Although Lapointe's book *Embracing the Earth's Wild Resources* is subtitled "a global conservation vision," it simply defends all commercial killing. Lapointe (2003: 155), convinced that the "Law of Nature" is "kill and be killed," seems driven by hatred of animals, opposing any initiative to protect them and defending every form of exploitation. His anthropocentric argument presents killing animals as sustainable use, promotes "free trade" of wildlife, praises elimination of sanctions on the killing of dolphins as collateral damage in the tuna-fishing industry, opposes a moratorium on whaling, supports every form of hunting, minimizes concern about endangered species and rejects the precautionary principle, the reasonable idea that we should be cautious about our environment, especially when we do not know all the facts or the effects of our actions. He attacks animal rights groups, charging them with illegal actions and with spreading misinformation, although Lapointe (2003: v) makes the "candid confession" that "it skipped my mind to note the various sources," meaning that his assertions are completely unsubstantiated. Considering even the corporate-friendly, pro-hunting World Wildlife Fund too radical, Lapointe inverts reality, describing animal rights groups as extremists and terrorists, armed with billions of dollars and dominating mass media, intent on victimizing industries, all of which tremble helplessly before their wealth and power.

Conservationist Killers

Hunters present themselves as conservationists motivated by ethical concerns but they focus on competition for status. Associations like the Boone and Crockett Club, the Pope and Young Club and the SCI maintain scoring systems for trophy animals and encourage members to kill more animals to obtain higher points. For example, hunters who kill individuals from every classification recognized by the Pope and Young Club are entered in record books for achieving the "North American Super Slam." Hunters spend hundreds of thousands of dollars to win such status.

Hunters claim to be conservationists, saying if they did not pay to kill them, animals would not survive because local people would have no financial incentive not to kill those animals themselves. Much of the money that hunting groups claim to spend on conservation actually goes to make killing animals more convenient, such as building roads and trails or clearing forests so "surplus" populations of prey species such as deer can be artificially maintained. While hunters claim to have increased populations of species such as caribou, deer or moose, this is achieved by killing predators such as wolves who normally would limit those populations.

Hunters say they follow natural laws. Yet, hunting, especially for sport, does not emulate natural predation in which weaker animals are killed and stronger ones survive. Sport hunters seek the biggest, strongest animals for trophies, leaving weaker ones to breed, thereby contributing to degeneration of species. They change the gender balance of animal populations by focusing on male animals, who can provide the most impressive trophies, such as large antlers and so on.

In addition to obviously harming individual animals, by killing the biggest, strongest animals for trophies, hunters have detrimental effects at the species level. *Newsweek* (Huang 2009) calls this "evolution in reverse," citing biologist Marco Festa-Bianchet from Quebec's University of Sherbrooke, whose studies of Alberta bighorn sheep found a 25 percent decline in horn size and size reductions in both male and female sheep due to hunters killing larger animals, leaving only smaller animals to reproduce. Hunting has the same impact on other species. For example, in Africa, it has led to more breeding by tuskless elephants, who are less prized by hunters. Festa-Bianchet says tusked elephants and larger bighorn sheep were "genetically 'better' individuals.… When you take them systematically out of the population for several years, you end up leaving essentially a bunch of losers doing the breeding."

Rather than preserving endangered species, hunters threaten their survival. Trophy hunters enjoy killing large carnivores, but these animals play an important role in keeping other species' numbers in check, thereby maintaining entire eco-systems. Killing top predators, such as wolves, starts a chain reaction that lets populations of deer, elk and other animals expand, stripping vegetation and threatening survival of many species.

Nevertheless, hunting means money. Gary A. Mauser (2004), professor emeritus at Simon Fraser University's Faculty of Business Administration, board member and former vice-president of the British Columbia Wildlife Federation, says provincial wildlife management programs are funded mainly by hunting licences. He defends sport hunting's economic importance, indicating that Canadian hunters spend $1.2 billion annually on hunting trips plus $1.5 billion on wildlife-related activities outside hunting season. A fervent opponent of gun-control and the Canadian government's gun-registry plan, Mauser is a member of the Canadian Firearms Advisory Committee for Public Safety Minister Stockwell Day. The *Toronto Star* (May 28, 2007) featured a photograph (now removed) from the Canadian National Firearms Association's website showing a grinning Mauser aiming a revolver at the camera and described the committee as "appointed and operating in virtual secrecy… made up almost entirely of pro-gun advocates opposed to the firearms registry."

In 2003, resident and non-resident hunters contributed $48 million to British Columbia's GDP, with freshwater angling contributing another $112 million. However, tourism activities not based on killing wildlife generated $5.1 billion (Service B.C. 2005). Thousands of non-resident sport hunters, mainly from the U.S. and Germany, accounted for higher revenues, since they spend thousands of dollars booking expeditions, in addition to transportation costs to areas where they can kill animals for trophies. Non-resident hunters pay different and higher costs including mandatory fees for guides and more expensive hunting licences, and killing rare species costs thousands of dollars.

Killing polar bears became a popular sport for wealthy sports hunters in the 1980s. About 15,000 of the world's estimated 20,000 to 25,000 polar bears live in Canada, the only country that permits killing them for sport. Hunting is restricted to Aboriginal people through a licence system and community quotas, but communities can sell their licences to sport hunters, who each pay tens of thousands of dollars for the opportunity to kill these animals. Inuit communities regard commercial polar bear hunting as a source of significant income.

American sport hunters who hunted polar bear in the N.W.T. spent an average of $37,699 for a hunting trip, plus $11,150 each for those who purchased taxidermy services (these costs are lower than those advertised on various outfitters' websites). Most also bought licences to kill other animals, especially musk-ox. Their main goal was obtaining trophies; most said they would not return to hunt in the N.W.T. if they were not allowed to import as trophies body parts of bears they had killed (Government of the Northwest Territories 2007)

In 2008, Canada's Environment Minister John Baird declared: "Our Government believes that the polar bear is an iconic symbol of Canada" (Palmer 2008). Yet, the Government does little to protect them. In its 2008 annual report, the Committee on the Status of Endangered Wildlife in Canada (COSEWIC) decided that despite serious threats from hunting and habitat loss, polar bears were not in "imminent" danger of extinction and designated them a species of "Special Concern," the weakest status and one they have had since 1991. The committee's report obligated Baird to create a management plan but only by 2014, by which time the Arctic's sea ice may have completely disappeared in summer (Carter 2008).

The U.S. banned imports of polar bear trophies under the *Marine Mammal Protection Act* from 1972–1994. After 1994, after extensive lobbying by hunting groups such as the SCI and the Canadian government, imports were allowed with permits from the U.S. Fish and Wildlife Service that indicated bears were killed under managed conditions. Members of hunting clubs like the SCI are eager to kill rare and endangered species and mobilize government support for their objectives. When the U.S. declared the polar bear a threatened species due to loss of sea ice due to global warming, Canadian government officials went to Washington D.C. to lobby for exemptions for polar bear hides. They said Inuit communities were economically dependent on money spent by U.S. hunters who visited northern Canada to kill polar bears. Bob McLeod, Minister of Industry, Tourism and Investment for the Northwest Territories, said the U.S. ban would stop hunting in that region, eliminating eighty-five jobs. McLeod said sport hunting was well-managed, monitored and sustainable and would have no effect on the polar bear population. In contrast, the U.S. Fish and Wildlife Service said polar bear habitat would be reduced by 50 percent by 2050, and the Sierra Club (which supports hunting) warned that polar bears were in grave danger. In 2005, the U.S. listed polar bears as threatened, again banning imports of trophies but not restricting oil and gas development although environmental groups called for such measures to protect bears and other wildlife. Sarah Palin, failed vice-presidential candidate and governor of Alaska, argued that listing of polar bears was not based on good scientific evidence and demanded reversal of that designation.

Most polar bears are killed in Nunavut, which increased quotas in 2005 against advice from scientists, who warned that bear populations are declining. Nunavut's government claimed bears were plentiful, based on numbers of sightings. Scientists responded that more bears are being sighted because more sea ice is melting, forcing bears to shore earlier. They warned that changing climate means bears will be unable to acquire enough fat to survive summer months of scarcity and the more extensive ice melting will force them to swim greater distances, with more risk of drowning. Two-thirds of the bear population will disappear by 2050, and they may become extinct in the next century. Northern governments and Inuit communities that derive financial benefits from hunting reject these warnings, assert that bears will adapt to climate change and oppose any restrictions.

In February 2009, wildlife protection groups, Alaska Wildlife Alliance, Oregon-based Big Wildlife and Canada's Raincoast Conservation asked online shopping site eBay to stop selling trophy hunts of grizzly and brown bears, black bears, wolves, cougars and other large predators on its website. In addition to online auction sales of clothing, electronics and used cars, the website advertised guided trophy hunts in Canada, the U.S. and abroad. The three groups oppose trophy hunting in Alaska and B.C. of brown bears and grizzly bears. The animals are threatened as their habitat is destroyed by logging, mining and other forms of energy extraction, as well as by urban growth and by the international trade in bear parts. Although grizzly bears are protected by the U.S. *Endangered Species Act*, they can be hunted in Alaska and Canada, where thousands are killed each year. Chris Genovali, executive director of British Columbia's Raincoast Conservation (2009) asked:

> Have the lives of Canada's grizzly bears, wolves and other large carnivores become so cheapened by the purveyors of trophy hunting that selling an opportunity to kill one is now as commonplace as trying to unload a used kitchen appliance or baseball cards on eBay?

Hunters say they are under attack from animal activists and

gun-control advocates. They claim that humans have always hunted and that these practices should be continued and even encouraged out of respect for tradition. However, cultures change and groups should not be frozen into archaic practices without other options. Furthermore, sport and subsistence hunting are different practices. As noted, appealing to tradition is a common strategy among people who exploit and abuse animals. Such arguments are obviously flawed and rarely accepted in other contexts. That such practices existed in the past is no justification for continuing harmful and violent activities such as rape or warfare. Hunting was a "tradition" in many societies but so was oppression of women; most agree such traditions are better abandoned.

5. CANADA'S SHAME

Images of Death

If one image, beyond red-coated Mounties, signifies Canada in the global imagination it is that of a man clubbing a seal to death on an ice floe. Unfortunately, Canadians are not recognized for enlightened treatment of animals but for cruelty towards them. Canada is notorious for its annual seal hunt, the world's largest slaughter of marine mammals. In reality, it is no "hunt" at all: sealers stride across the ice to newborn seals who cannot escape and beat them to death or shoot them. The repugnance that millions around the world feel towards these activities helped build a global animal protection movement. Many eminent scientists, artists and celebrities express opposition to the practice, bringing international attention to what is rightly called "Canada's Shame."

Most Canadians, too, are repelled by the annual slaughter that stains the ice and their own reputations. In 2008, Ipsos Reid reported that only 39 percent of Canadians support it. Journalist Peter Worthington (2008) compared it to mass executions committed by the Nazis and Saddam Hussein and to genocidal acts in Srebrenica and Cambodia, concluding it is "demeaning" to kill animals in mass numbers for "little reason." Novelist Timothy Findlay called it "degrading... both to the character and to the stature of a brilliant, caring culture." The fact that these comments apply equally as much to other forms of exploitation, such as using animals for food, does not make the seal hunt any more acceptable, although proponents claim as much.

The slaughter is not only barbaric and cruel towards individual animals but is based on dubious estimates of seal populations and threatens the ocean's broader ecosystems and, ultimately, human society itself. It is not necessary for human survival and is premised on selling seals' skins as luxury fashion items. Failing markets for fur mean the industry is of only marginal economic significance. Nevertheless, a few Canadians refuse to let these practices properly fade away as the anachronisms they are. Unfortunately, they have been supported in this by successive Canadian governments and by all Canadian political parties, except the Greens. The Conservative Party is notorious for opposition to anti-cruelty laws so its support for the seal hunt is unsurprising, as is that of the Liberal Party (Dion 2008), which endorses activities they call "sustainable, humane and commercially viable… a time-honoured tradition and an important industry… a valuable link to Canadian cultural heritage." Perhaps most craven was the NDP, which in 2003 fired Rick Smith as leader Jack Layton's chief of staff when Newfoundland NDP leader Jack Harris complained of Smith's previous work as executive director of the International Fund for Animal Welfare (IFAW), which opposes the seal hunt.

Humane Killing

Trying to make the slaughter seem less barbaric, the Canadian government announced new regulations in December 2008, including guidelines stating that sealers should ensure animals were dead before skinning them. That this should have to be specified and that it is presented as a "humane" advancement is indicative of the brutality involved. Another regulation directed sealers not to use spiked clubs, or hakipiks, on seals older than a year unless the seals were shot first. However, only a few seals older than a year are killed, so these regulations make little difference and are merely propaganda to make the hunt seem "humane." The government enjoined sealers to wait one minute before skinning an animal. Sealers, demonstrating their "humane" concern for animals, protested that this new requirement would slow their operations. How the regulations would be enforced remained unclear. The government was said to be "considering" surveillance cameras on helicopters and an anonymous tip-line so sealers could report offenders. Given the sealers' commitment to killing as many animals as possible and their violent hatred of ideas about animal protection, expecting them to report one another's violations is fantasy. In any case, sealers simply ignored the guidelines. Observing the slaughter, Rebecca Aldworth (2008), director of Animal Programs for Humane Society International, stated:

> Yesterday we filmed sealers consistently violating the few regulations that exist to protect seals. It is no coincidence that today the Canadian government is doing everything in its power to stop us from documenting the slaughter. The DFO [Department of Fisheries and Oceans] will only allow one of our helicopters to go into the hunt area, preventing more than a dozen journalists from witnessing the killing today. If the Canadian government's claims that this is a humane slaughter are true, then why are they working so hard to hide it?
>
> Not one sealer I saw yesterday was obeying the new conditions of their hunting licenses — to stun the seals, check for unconsciousness, and then bleed the animals. Given that the sealers are flagrantly ignoring the rules in front of us, imagine what happens when our cameras aren't there.

Describing the cruelty, the International Federation for Animal Welfare (2008a) reported:

> IFAW documents the seal hunt for a few days a year and

we can only be filming one boat at time. Yet every year we see animals being shot or clubbed and left to suffer. We see animals hooked and skinned alive, as we did yesterday. The most striking image from yesterday's footage involved a seal that was injured and then hooked in the face and dragged back to the boat. We were moving between boats and came across a sealer on the ice with what appeared to be a dead seal. He started writing in the snow with a bloody finger; the message was "F@ck [sic] Off."

As we were circling to get a better shot of his message to us, the seal that was on the ice behind him, tried to sit up! This was clearly not swimming reflex, this animal was still conscious. The sealer did not respond by taking action to quickly kill the seal as required by the Marine Mammal Regulations, instead he hooked it in the face and then proceeded to drag the animal across the ice and onto the boat, still alive.

In 2008, the Humane Society of the United States estimated that over one million seals were killed in the previous four years. Numbers may be higher, since many are wounded and slip into the water where they are not recovered and thus not counted. The Canadian government insists that the hunt is sustainable and sets quotas for each year's kill. However, critics say quotas are determined without objective population surveys and that sealers violate them with impunity.

While Canada's government and sealers say the hunt is humane and sustainable, common sense suggests and evidence shows exactly the opposite. Actions we consider humane are those marked by compassion, sympathy and consideration. None of these describe the process of hunting generally and to apply the term to the brutality of the annual seal slaughter so rightly condemned by international opinion is to enter a surreal world where words lose all meaning. The impact on the oceans' ecosystem of killing huge numbers of seals is still unknown, but decades of fishing in the area devastated the cod population as the industry destroyed itself. No evidence suggests industries will regulate themselves and operate with the "sustainable" methods they claim to practice. Rather, the logic of capitalism demands short-term profits no matter what long-term costs ensue.

Recognizing the hunt's brutality, the European Commission proposed banning import and trade of seal products in the European Union, a move that would help eliminate markets, drive prices for seal pelts even lower and hasten the end of these practices. The Canadian government undertook a furious lobbying campaign to prevent the ban. Ignoring strong domestic and international popular opinion and scientific evidence, the DFO remains zealously committed to sealing. The DFO (2005) website claims to refute "myths" created by animal protection groups. Instead, it reveals government duplicity in misleading the public. The DFO claims opponents play on sentiment by using images of cute baby seals with white coats and says they are no longer hunted:

> The image of the whitecoat harp seal is used prominently by seal hunt opponents. This image gives the false impression that vulnerable whitecoat pups are targeted by sealers during the commercial hunt.
>
> Harp seals can be legally hunted once they have moulted their white coat, which occurs at about 12–14 days of age. However, they are not usually hunted until they reach the "beater" stage of development at around 25 days old.

Only intense international outrage led the government to stop the killing of whitecoat seals in 1987, and it was undertaken only as a propaganda effort to make slaughter seem acceptable. Although their coats may have changed colour, it is misleading to claim that these seals are no longer babies. A twelve-day-old seal is not an adult (and killing adults is no more acceptable in any case). Almost all seals killed each year are under a month old and have not had their first swim or solid meal. Every year, animal protection groups and international media document the suffering created by sealers, who club, impale and shoot vulnerable baby seals and skin them while they are still alive.

Although up to half of seals are skinned alive, the DFO calls this a humane operation and praises sealers' use of the hakipik:

> Hunting methods were studied by the Royal Commission on Seals and Sealing in Canada and it found that the clubbing of seals, when properly performed, is at least as humane as, and often more humane than, the killing methods used in commercial slaughterhouses, which are accepted by the majority of the public.

Politicians repeated assertions that killing methods are as humane as those used in commercial slaughterhouses. In March 2006, Newfoundland and Labrador Premier Danny Williams, debating musician Paul McCartney and Heather Mills McCartney on CNN's *Larry King Live*, made this claim (while suggesting that animal protection groups such as IFAW, Greenpeace and PETA were subjects of FBI terrorism investigations). Given the horrifying conditions in slaughterhouses, the government's claims may be true but this is no defence of sealing. Rather, it is a further reason to condemn it. Many who oppose killing seals also oppose slaughtering other animals, and, doubtless, others who are sickened and outraged by the seal slaughter's obvious cruelty may be encouraged to reflect on the consistency of their ethical principles and to oppose other forms of animal abuse. In this sense, the government is more consistent in its readiness to defend any form of animal exploitation if profits can be made. This is exemplified by an internal Agriculture Department memo obtained by the Canadian Press (Rennie 2009) in which government officials advised Agriculture Minister Gerry Ritz not to follow Europe, the United States and Europe in banning cat and dog fur from entering Canada, despite widespread public opposition, because "a ban could have implications for the farmed fur industry in Canada and for Canada's position against the banning of Canadian seal products by other countries." Yet even in economic terms alone, the hunt is senseless.

Economics of Sealing

The DFO's website claims sealing is economically significant:

> Seals are a significant source of income. For some individual sealers and for thousands of families in Eastern Canada at a time of year when other fishing options are limited at best, sealing can represent as much as 35 per cent of a sealer's annual income in some coastal communities.

However, Sea Shepherd Conservation Society (SSCS) (n.d.) challenges this, using the government's own statistics to show that only about 6,000 people receive income from sealing, a limited, highly subsidized industry, and that some sealers make under $1,000, although it notes that "former federal Fisheries Minister John Crosbie is a millionaire heir to the fortunes made from the Crosbie Sealing Company." Essentially, commercial seal hunting is a make-work project for fishers in the off-season. Although it is extremely costly to maintain and a substantial drain on Canadian taxpayers, the government continues to bolster this unsustainable industry and to issue deceptive statements. For example, the DFO claims:

> DFO does not subsidize the seal hunt. Sealing is an economically viable industry. All subsidies ceased in 2001. Even before that time, any subsidies provided were for market and product development, including a meat subsidy, to encourage full use of the seal. In fact, government has provided much less subsidization to the sealing industry than recommended by the Royal Commission on Seals and Sealing.

In fact, subsidies are provided to the industry by the Canadian public through their government. As SSCS observes, substantial subsidies are provided by federal and provincial governments in the form of surveillance and locating seals for the sealers, icebreaking ships that permit sealers to reach the seals, Coast Guard search-and-rescue operations, regulatory costs, market research and extensive lobbying and public relations activities, meaning that the hunt costs more to taxpayers than it makes. Even if one does not oppose the hunt on the grounds of basic decency and compassion towards animals, strong economic arguments exist against it. In the *National Post* (Teitel 2008), Toronto lawyer Murray Teitel outlines astronomical costs to taxpayers involved in defending the hunt: deploying Canadian Coast Guard vessels, including icebreakers, helicopters and patrol planes to assist sealers to reach the animals or to rescue sealers when they become lost or trapped in the ice, mounting efforts to oppose bans on imports of seal products and on raising challenges at the World Trade Organization (jeopardizing relationships with countries that import other Canadian goods), sending expensive delegations of politicians on largely unsuccessful lobbying tours to Europe and maintaining an army of bureaucrats at the DFO to defend the hunt against international criticism and oversee its operations. Additionally, the government spends hundreds of thousands of dollars annually blocking international observers from documenting the hunt. Teitel notes the costs of the international boycott against Canadian seafood organized by the Humane Society of the United States (HSUS) and other groups with the objective of convincing the Canadian fishing industry to stop participating in and supporting the annual commercial seal hunt. The boycott caused a 44 percent drop in 2007 of snow crab exports alone, the major seafood export from the provinces where sealing occurs, at a cost of $465 million. The HSUS persuaded over five thousand businesses to observe the boycott, meaning hundreds of millions more dollars of lost profits as the government defends a practice that creates less than 1 percent of the value of the provinces' fishing industry. Adding these and other costs, Teitel finds Canadian taxpayers pay at least ten times as much each year as the sealing industry generates and concludes that this is "a colossal waste of taxpayers' money" that could be better spent to train sealers for jobs suited to contemporary economy, rather than "preserv[ing] them as relics of a hunter/gatherer one."

It is not only animal protection groups that oppose the slaughter. For example, in a November 16, 2005, letter to then-Prime Minister Paul Martin, Edward Kangas (Humane Society of the United States 2005), formerly global chair and CEO of Deloitte & Touche and, at the time of his letter, chair of the National Multiple Sclerosis Society of the United States and a member of the boards of directors of four New York Stock Exchange companies, outlined the economic case for ending the commercial seal hunt (also noting that "many rightly oppose the commercial slaughter of seals for ethical or conservation measures"). Kangas pointed out that not only had tens of millions of people around the world endorsed the boycott against Canadian seafood products but major corporate distributors of Canadian seafood had joined it as well. A major target is Canadian snow crab, representing half the value of Newfoundland's fishery. Kangas observes:

> since the boycott began, the total value of Canadian snow crab exports to the U.S. has declined by over $156 million — a 36 percent drop and nearly ten times the value of the seal hunt… multimillion-dollar losses were reported at the leading fishing company on Canada's east coast — Fisheries Products International. The company lost about $7.4 million during the three quarters of this year, while it earned a net profit of $10.7 million during the same period in 2004.

Noting that only a few thousand people, commercial fishers who, on average, obtain under 5 percent of their incomes from sealing, participate in commercial sealing and that profits from that activity are insignificant, Kangas declares himself "astounded" at the situation and at the government's policy of propping up this industry:

> I and other leaders in the business community are amazed that Canada would allow its international reputation and fishing industry to be so heavily compromised for this economically marginal activity. It is even more surprising when one considers that as the seafood boycott gains momentum, global markets for seal products are closing (as evidenced by recent European initiatives). Moreover, the damage to Canada's international reputation and economy is growing exponentially. While the boycott focuses primarily on Canadian seafood and snow crabs, more and more people are now dispensing with tourism and other Canadian products.

Government Defence of a Dying Industry

The DFO website identifies "Myth #8: The seal hunt is loosely monitored and DFO doesn't punish illegal hunting activity or practices" and claims that sealers who do not observe the rules are penalized. However, penalties are minor, exemplified by the case of Mark Small. In January 2009, one of Canada's longest legal cases ended with a conviction of ten sealers for illegally selling blueback seal pelts in 1996. A larger group of 101 sealers was originally charged, and most were convicted but a few fought the charges. One, Mark Small, told the court that discussions with the DFO convinced him that the 1993 regulations were not being enforced. CBC News (2009a) quoted Small: "I think everybody was fully aware that DFO had turned a blind eye to the activities that were taking place in 1996." Small said a government inspector helped him locate the seals and that DFO officials inspected his boat four times, ignoring his catch of blueback seals (Smyth 2009). The court concluded that Small knew he was breaking the law despite the fact that the DFO was not enforcing it. Despite his conviction, Small was selected for the government's delegation to Europe to lobby against the European Parliament's proposed ban on importation of seal products and was even presented as a "model sealer," according to the IFAW.

While the DFO encourages sealers to break the law and the government rewards them with international junkets, police harass animal advocates. In March 2006, the Royal Canadian Mounted Police and DFO charged five observers for coming too close to sealing activity. Canada's bizarrely named Seal Protection Regulations makes it a crime to observe and document the killing of seals without a government permit, which prohibits any approach closer than 10 metres to sealers engaged in killing. Under this Orwellian legislation, witnessing killings without a permit is punishable by a $100,000 fine or a year in prison. The police and DFO are far less diligent in arresting sealers who assault observers or in investigating violations committed by sealers. Clearly, the laws are intended to block observers from documenting cruelties inflicted by sealers, while police facilitate the hunt and overlook violence committed against observers and protestors.

In March 2008, the Canadian Coast Guard icebreaker *Des Groseilliers* twice rammed the SSCS ship *Farley Mowat* to stop crew members from observing the hunt. On April 4, a mob of sealers assaulted the *Farley Mowat*'s crew; the ship was berthed in St. Pierre awaiting resumption of the slaughter, which had been suspended after four sealers drowned when their vessel capsized while being towed by the Coast Guard. While police watched, rock-throwing, axe-wielding sealers attacked the crew, cut the ship's mooring lines and threw its gangplank in the water, setting it adrift in the harbour, where it was in danger of crashing onto rocks or nearby ships. The captain was forced to cold-start the engines, risking serious damage, to avoid collision. On April 12, the Coast Guard sent armed troops to board the *Farley Mowat*, confiscate all photographic documentation of the hunt and arrest its crew, despite the fact that the Dutch-registered ship was in international waters. Then Fisheries Minister Loyola Hearn described this as protection of sealers although the

SSCS questioned why sealers needed protection and maintained that the real reason for the assault on their ship was to distract attention from the Coast Guard's incompetence in the death of the four sealers.

After the ship was illegally impounded, it was held at the expense of Canadian taxpayers, accruing substantial costs, as the government attempted to auction the ship but was unable to find a buyer for the decrepit vessel. Although SSCS successfully sued the DFO for a previous seizure, of *Sea Shepherd II*, between 1983 and 1985, Watson said the *Farley Mowat* was due for retirement and the government's action saved SSCS those costs. In September 2009, the government fined two SSCS crew members, Captain Alex Cornelissen of the Netherlands and First Officer Peter Hammarstedt of Sweden, $45,000 for simply observing the slaughter, denying them the right to attend the trial because it had deported them earlier and refused to allow them to return to speak in their own defence. Cornelissen scoffed at the verdict:

> The Canadian government continues to take extreme measures to prevent people from exposing their most horrific secret, the largest marine wildlife slaughter on the planet. Boarding our Dutch registered vessel in international waters at gunpoint couldn't prevent us from getting evidence to the European parliament that this so-called hunt is nothing short of a biological holocaust and the sealers, nothing but sadistic butchers. The amount of the fine is totally irrelevant as even a one million dollar fine would not impress us as we did nothing wrong, we are not the ones committing crimes against nature. And since we are inadmissible into Canada mentioning a jail sentence in lieu of a fine is nothing but a final sputter from the bureaucrats who can't admit defeat. Paying the fine is the last thing on my mind. The hunt is virtually over; there is no longer a market. We may have lost the battle in court but we won the war to ban seal products.

Defending the hunt, DFO repeatedly cites on its website, in press releases and various public statements a single report published in the *Canadian Veterinary Journal* (Daoust, Crook, Bollinger, Campbell and Wong 2002), arguing that the majority of seals are killed in an "acceptably humane manner" comparable to the processing of livestock in slaughterhouses.

In fact, the report cited is not peer-reviewed, nor is it the Canadian Veterinary Medical Association's official position, as the government suggested (Lavigne 2005: fn1). Furthermore, the five "independent veterinarians" create a misleading impression. Their observations were made aboard sealing vessels, meaning sealers were aware of their presence and that they were being monitored for the purpose of reporting on the hunt. Nevertheless, the veterinarians still observed live seals brought aboard. Lavigne (2) notes:

> The number of seals arriving on the deck of a sealing vessel (dead or alive) is not a measure of whether the seals were killed in an "acceptably humane manner." Such determination can only be made at the location of the killing (either by direct observation, or by post-mortem examination). Only in extreme cases of negligence (such as those apparently observed on 3 occasions by [the veterinarians]) would one expect to find a seal still alive and conscious on the deck of a sealing vessel. Such seals almost certainly would have been struck with a club, a hakipik, or some illegal weapon like a boat hook or gaff; hooked while still conscious; dragged across the ice floes for some distance; hoisted onto the ship (using the hook imbedded, most likely, in its jaw or eye socket); and thrown onto the deck of the ship. Incidents like these characterize some of the worst examples of cruelty associated with the Canadian seal hunt. The fact that [the veterinarians] observed 3 such cases in 167 observations (involving sealers who were aware they were being observed) underscores the inherent and continuing cruelty of the hunt.

In contrast, an international panel of veterinarians found extensive evidence of "considerable and unacceptable suffering," suggesting that up to 42 percent of seals examined were alive and conscious while being skinned. For this report, sealers were not aware they would be observed. Video footage taken from a helicopter showed that many seals were killed by illegal methods, that in 79 percent of cases sealers did not check for signs of life as required, that 40 percent were shot or clubbed but not killed immediately and were left to suffer, and that many were hooked, bled or skinned alive. Although the Canadian veterinarians presented their observations in such a way as to provide support for the hunt, it is clear that, additionally, the DFO used their report in a deceptive manner. One veterinarian, Pierre Ives Daoust from Charlottetown's Atlantic Veterinary College, was later hired to run workshops for sealers on "humane" killing ("first smashing the skull, then feeling the skull to make sure it is crushed, and then bleeding the animal"), organized by the Fur Institute of Canada and paid for by the Newfoundland and Quebec governments (CBC News (2009b). Having one's skull crushed does not meet standard definitions of "humane" treatment.

Canada's government lies to the public and wastes taxpayers' money to defend a dying industry condemned by most of the world. In 2009 Russian Prime Minister Vladimir Putin announced an end to that country's seal hunt, calling it a "bloody industry" that should have been banned long ago: Russia's Natural Resources Minister, Yury Trutnyev, called it "one of the most inhumane types of hunting in the world, which is banned in the vast majority of developed states" (Moore 2009). In March, Canadian Senator Mac Harb introduced a bill to end the commercial hunt; although it presented an opportunity to end this particular barbarism, other senators rallied to defend sealing. The government remained committed to the industry, using standard tactics of pretended concern for Indigenous people to defend commercial slaughter conducted by non-Natives. In 2009, Governor-General Michelle Jean, later followed by Stephen Harper and several Cabinet members made a media-show of consuming seal-flesh in Nunavut, supposedly demonstrating concern for Indigenous people when their real object was defence of the East Coast commercial fur industry, not subsistence hunting. When the European Union announced in 2009 that it would ban marketing of seal products, the government said it would raise a trade challenge at the World Trade Organization, estimated to cost about $10 million to defend the $1 million industry. Unsurprisingly, the fur industry remains ready to spend unlimited millions of taxpayers' dollars to defend its own profits.

6. RELICS OF BARBARISM

Spectacles of Domination

Capitalist production often conceals animal exploitation, locating slaughterhouses and factory farms in rural or low-income areas and restricting access to vivisection laboratories, surrounding them with surveillance and security forces. However, other forms of exploitation become profit-generating spectacles, sold as entertainment. For example, the Calgary Stampede is a major tourist attraction and symbol of Canada. Like all rodeos, it is promoted as rugged competition between "man" and beast, involving displays of skill and courage, and as a worthy but entertaining tradition. In reality, rodeos are demonstrations of power and control, based on ideas of dominion over nature, characterized by animal abuse and motivated by greed. Such spectacles reinforce ideological understandings of human relationships to animals, naturalizing hierarchy and domination. Presented as family entertainment, suitable for children, the lessons they teach are of brutality and cruelty, socializing children to accept inequality and abuse. Dr. Eleonora Gullone, chair of the Australian Psychological Society's interest group Psychologists for the Promotion of Animal Welfare (2006), states:

> Whilst animal welfare is a major concern as seen by the blatantly cruel behaviour toward the badly injured bull, the message that is being communicated to the public is of

even more serious concern…. Marketing rodeos as family entertainment is a big concern from a psychological point of view. In particular, communicating the message to children that it is fun to battle with a frightened and distressed animal teaches them that the suffering of other living beings is a source of entertainment and enjoyment.

Human performers demonstrate mastery over nature and animals by racing and chasing them, roping them, wrestling them to the ground and triumphantly binding them. Animals are provoked — tormented, hit, shocked with electronic prods, straps are jerked tight around horses' sensitive flanks to make them buck — to make them seem "wild" and thus more entertaining to audiences watching them struggle or attempting to escape. Many are injured, suffering bruises and broken bones, or killed. Terrified calves fleeing their tormentors are roped and jerked violently to the ground; many suffer broken necks. Other animals are killed in racing events.

Abusers regularly claim to "love" their victims, and rodeo organizers and participants are no exception. Although rodeos and the "skills" they celebrate are derived from the livestock industry, which slaughters billions of animals annually, and rodeo events involve deliberate cruelty, proponents claim to care for animals. Yet, for them, animals are simply profit-generating machines. In fact, in the U.S., the Professional Rodeo Cowboys Association (PRCA) and the International Pro Rodeo Association opposed legislation banning slaughter of horses because the industry wants to profit even from those horses it has "used up" by selling them to slaughterhouses when they can no longer perform.

Cowboy Images and Invented Tradition

The rodeo's protagonist is the cowboy. Cowboys are not very significant in Canadian history; they played a greater role in the U.S., but even there the "cowboy period" only lasted a few decades in the nineteenth century. The cowboy image is filtered through mass media, with mythical associations added by Hollywood, especially during the 1950s Cold War period, when cowboy images proliferated as signs of courageous masculine strength, self-reliance and rightwing political values. Lawrence (1981) describes the rodeo as a ritualized re-enactment of the Myth of the West, the aggressive and exploitative taming of the frontier through domination of animals, subjugation of nature and conquest of Indigenous populations. Lawrence links these with values of ancient Judaeo-Christian pastoralist societies, but they are also fundamental to the expansion of capitalism. Cowboys adopt a code of individualism, courage, anti-intellectualism, stoicism and disregard for pain, qualities valorized in the rodeo's ritualized sado-masochism, complete with eroticized costuming, pain, ropes and bondage. The cowboy image is also associated with conservative values and has been a regular element of political propaganda, adopted by U.S. presidents such as Reagan and Bush. During the Cold War period, the Calgary Stampede featured Hollywood actors who portrayed cowboys on television and used them to celebrate a mythical West that never existed. Stampede "tradition" has less to do with local history than with Hollywood's militant, patriarchal Cold War cowboy. Militaristic associations are direct, as the Stampede includes military displays including tanks, aircraft and weapons. From the 2009 Stampede, Global TV's website ran a photo of Canadian General Walt Natynczyk waving his cowboy hat while astride a torpedo in a display "reminiscent of the famous climactic scene in the classic movie *Catch 22*," watched by U.S. General David Petraeus, Commander of Central Command. (In fact, the film is *Dr. Strangelove*; the scene depicts Slim Pickens as super-patriot Major "King" Kong, whooping and waving his cowboy hat while straddling a nuclear-bomb dropped from a B52 over Russia, which in turn triggers a Russian Doomsday Weapon that destroys nearly all life on earth; what Natynczyk intended by his performance can only be guessed.)

Costumes are derived from Hollywood films, not Alberta history. The cowboy is a marketing tool, used to construct fantasies of the past for commercial purposes and to enlist adherence to militaristic, patriarchal ideology. Through this image, nostalgia for a largely invented past is superimposed on other events such as ordinary midway rides operating at the Calgary Exhibition. The myth also fits Alberta's ideology of capitalism, with its themes of individualism and risk-taking and its view of the environment as simply a repository of resources to be exploited.

Self-named "the Greatest Outdoor Show on Earth," the Stampede is a triumph of marketing. Although presented as a celebration of tradition, that tradition is an invented one, in which recent practices are accepted as having deep roots in the past and by which groups justify themselves through asserting links with the past where none exist (Hobsbawm and Ranger 1992). The Stampede celebrates Calgary's "cowboy heritage" but these aspects of ranch-life existed only briefly in Calgary's history and have little connection with contemporary realities of agribusiness. Some events may have developed from contests staged by bored rural workers, and local ranchers engaged in the horse-racing business sometimes added western dress as a comic touch to events, but a prolonged advertising campaign transformed these aspects into the Stampede's central symbols (Foran 2008).

Raymond, Alberta, claims to have held Canada's first rodeo in 1901, and interest in cowboys was stirred by touring American Wild West shows, but at the time, rodeos had little attraction. Animal welfare concerns mixed with efforts to reject the primitive associations of ranching and to demonstrate that Alberta was becoming civilized. In 1905 the *Calgary Herald* expressed "disgust" at a steer-wrestling show. In 1910, the *Morning Albertan* dismissed the rodeo as "a thing of the past" (Foran 2008: 5). In 1911 the editors of the *Fort McLeod Advertiser* described a rodeo there as a "relic of barbarism" and condemned it in terms still applicable today:

> When unwilling beasts have to be goaded and frightened into action and are ridden about with blood from the spurs

dripping from their flanks, the whole outfit responsible for
the "show" should be hauled up for cruelty to animals.
(quoted in Wetherell 2008: 29)

In Calgary, the Stampede started in 1912 and merged in 1923 with
the Exhibition, which had operated since 1896. American vaudeville
performer and cowboy Guy Weadic persuaded Calgary business
owners with investments in ranching, meatpacking and a brewery
that a rodeo could be a money-making operation. They began a
marketing campaign, using large cash prizes to draw contestants,
coordinating events with a visit from the governor general and per-
suading the railroad to offer reduced fares. Complaints about cruelty
were raised right at the start, with outraged descriptions of wounded
animals, but local businesses were thrilled by an influx of customers,
and the city government quickly recognized potential profits.

Rather than growing from a local rodeo tradition, the Stampede
encouraged its development. Once it became evident that money
could be made, rodeos were staged in surrounding towns. By
the 1920s, rodeo was recognized as a sport and by the 1940s the
Stampede was a significant event. Now, major corporations like
Coca-Cola, Starbucks, Dodge, AT&T and others sponsor rodeos,
purchasing stereotyped images of masculinity and patriarchal "family
values" associated with domination of animals.

Over the years, the Stampede continued to spin off other money-
making ventures such as sporting events, concerts, trade shows,
animal auctions and biotechnology sales, supplementing them with
parades, pancake breakfasts, blacksmith contests, marching bands,
military displays, fireworks, visits from television stars and royalty
and contests such as Meadow Muffin Madness, in which cows are
encouraged to defecate on coloured squares in Stephen Avenue
Mall. Recognizing the profits to be made from the Stampede and
its spin-offs, Calgary media long ago stopped criticizing the vulgar-
ity of such events and now promote them, often using stereotyped
western lingo.

Opposing Rodeo Cruelty

What is unchanged is the cruelty to animals that has plagued the event from its inception. Animal protection groups have long opposed abuse as entertainment and have achieved some victories. Rodeos are banned entirely in the U.K., and the Netherlands does not allow U.S.-style events. Several cities in Australia, Brazil, New Zealand and the U.S. also banned rodeos. Major U.S. cities dropped events such as calf-roping, flank straps, electronic shocking devices, hooks, whips and spurs. In 2006, following efforts by the Vancouver Humane Society (VHS), Vancouver City Council banned all rodeos there, the first Canadian city to take this progressive decision. The VHS, along with the B.C. SPCA and Liberation B.C. also persuaded Cloverdale Rodeo to ban four of its most brutal events: calf roping, steer wrestling, team roping and "cowboy cow milking." (In this activity, riders rope a cow, dismount their horses and swarm the terrified animal, one grabbing her head while another attempts to squeeze milk from her udder into a bottle.) The ban came after activists protested on the rodeo field and one day after a calf was killed in a roping event.

Aware of Vancouver's decision to ban rodeos and with their contract up for renewal, organizers feared their activities might be stopped entirely, and some activists argued that banning the most obviously brutal events actually saved the rodeo, allowing it to continue abusing and exploiting animals. Nevertheless, as Cloverdale Rodeo explained on its website, the decision caused "a firestorm" among the "rodeo community" and resulted in Cloverdale Rodeo losing its sanctions with both the Canadian and American rodeo associations, meaning competitors would no longer earn points towards the Canadian Finals Rodeo and the U.S. National Finals Rodeo in Las Vegas. Both associations sought to discipline Cloverdale Rodeo for what they considered a concession to animal advocacy groups. To attract competitors, Cloverdale Rodeo increased its prize money to $360,000 in 2008, making it the second largest pay-out in Canada, fifth in North America. Following Cloverdale's decision to drop some forms of abuse, the VHS approached another of B.C.'s large rodeos, in Abbotsford, appealing to the better impulses of the area's large Christian population with a poster depicting rodeo cruelties and text reading: "The words of Jesus speak of kindness, mercy and compassion. A far cry from the values on display in rodeos, where fear, pain and distress are used to make animals perform for human amusement."

The VHS poster emphasized the concern for animals that has been a marginalized tendency in Christian theology, one over-shadowed by mainstream emphasis on dominion and the idea that animals exist for human use. Few Christians seemed willing to apply their Golden Rule to animals. Rodeo organizers denounced the post-ers as "shocking" and "in quite poor taste." Pastor Stacey O'Neill, of Abbotsford's Olivet Mennonite Church, banned them from his church and defended the rodeo:

> They're definitely extreme and are grabbing people's atten-tion, but I think they're uncalled for…. Most people realize there's a definite distinction between cruelty to animals and a rodeo; they don't coincide. We even have some people in our church involved in the rodeo; if anybody has a love for animals, it's these people. They make sure they are treated with the most care and respect. (Sinoski 2008)

O'Neill's ideas of "care and respect" conflict with videotaped evi-dence of cruelty at rodeos documented by the U.S. animal protection group SHARK (Showing Animals Respect and Kindness) and other groups, readily accessible on YouTube. However, they correspond with attitudes of other Christians, such as evangelical cowboy churches, which are proliferating across North America. Identifying with western heritage and offering sermons about trail rides and bap-tisms in horse-troughs, these churches organize their own rodeos. For example, Arizona-based rodeo announcer Coy Huffman's Cowboy

Church International and Pro Rodeo Ministries spreads his doctrine at the Xtreme Bible Rodeo Camp. Linked with the cowboy church movement, and with evangelical groups in Ukraine, is Sweden's western-themed Kingdom Center Church, which was accused in 2008 of cult-like behaviour, forced child labour and conducting violent exorcisms. The image of the crusading Christian cowboy was an important symbol in George Bush's presidency, as it was for Ronald Reagan and Theodore Roosevelt. A rodeo fan, Bush created a National Day of the Cowboy in 2005, linking the cowboy symbol with his own political agenda.

While Vancouver recognized rodeos as "relic[s] of barbarism" and banned them, in 2008, Toronto stepped backward as the Canadian National Exhibition (CNE) welcomed its first rodeo in over a quarter-century. Sponsored by Dodge corporation, the event prompted *Toronto Star* columnist Bill Taylor (2008) to enthuse "Yee-haw, the Rodeo's Back!" and to accept the Rodeo Management Group's claims that the animals are well cared for. Also in 2008 Toyota corporation sponsored the Ontario Toyota Dealers Royal Rodeo Day at Toronto's Royal Agricultural Winter Fair, advertised on the fair's website as being "all about family." Despite letters pointing out that the company's reputation would not be improved by animal abuse, Toyota continued its sponsorship in 2009. Other Ontario cities attempt to profit from spectacles of animal cruelty, making no pretence of drawing on tradition. For example, claiming that their sporadically held rodeo constituted a "world class event," Markham's Board of Trade simply incorporated Calgary's advertising slogans for its own website while announcing its goal of "generating money into our local business economy."

Needing to recruit new audiences for institutionalized cruelty, rodeo organizers target children. Like the hunting lobby, they recognize that, unless indoctrinated when young to see animal cruelty as entertainment, few people will be interested in such practices. In Prince George, West of the Rockies Pro Rodeo Finals organized a special mini-rodeo free to all elementary-school students and distributed tickets to schools. The mini-rodeo featured all the events of the regular rodeo, including events banned at Cloverdale Rodeo and elsewhere, accompanied by claims from rodeo organizers and participants that "rodeo is not cruel to animals." Nearly a thousand children received coupons for half-price admission to the regular rodeo events, provided that full-price adult admissions were purchased as well (Clarke 2008).

Rather than opposing animal cruelty, politicians use the Calgary Stampede as a photo opportunity, flipping pancakes and dressing in western costumes. In 2008, Alberta Liberal leader Kevin Taft donned western gear to introduce a private member's motion recognizing rodeo as Alberta's official sport. Although Taft received majority support, Culture Minister Lindsay Blackett argued that other sports were equally deserving and rodeo should not have special status.

The absurdities and ethical backwardness of the Calgary Stampede, well recognized at its inception, are even more apparent in the twenty-first century. Certainly, anyone inspired by Gandhi's aphorism to search for Canada's moral greatness will find no signpost in Calgary, except among those who call for termination of this abusive spectacle.

7. PETS AND PRISONERS

A Pet-Loving Nation

A 2007 Ipsos Reid poll for the Canadian Animal Health Institute counted approximately 7.9 million cats and 5.9 million dogs in Canada. Among Canadian households, 35 percent have a dog and 38 percent have a cat. Many feel emotional bonds with animals, sometimes more than with other humans. Supplying pets with food, toys, equipment and various products is a $4.5 billion-per-year market. Spending on pets increased from $277 per household in 1999 to $377 in 2005. Pet-related industries are expanding, including veterinarians, dog walkers, groomers, trainers, therapists, pet insurance, photography, portraits, books, designer clothing, furniture and waste-removal services. Joining magazines like *Dogs in Canada*, *Bark* and *Urban Dog*, *Modern Dog* advises on "How to Update Your Dog's Spring Wardrobe" (Spring 2006) or "Green Doggy Styles" (Fall 2007). Pet industries describe a booming trend they term the humanization of animals, while media regularly warn of excessive concern for animals.

Clearly, pet-keeping matters to Canadians in economic, social and psychological terms. However, our manner of acquiring and disposing of pets is a form of commodity fetishism, in which breeding organizations and pet industries treat animals as commodities and assign them a particular value, responding to faddish demands for particular types, often in response to popular films or in emulation of celebrity tastes. Purchasing certain animal-commodities, such as "pure breeds" or dogs bred for fighting, is a means by which consumers acquire social status and construct personal identities through projection onto these animals of special qualities. Capitalism's magic system allows owners of purebred or fierce animals to imagine that they themselves embody the power of these commodities, displaying their own taste, power or masculinity through the ownership of these animals. Social class is marked by aesthetic choices that allow depiction of status; class fractions develop specific aesthetic criteria, expressed in tastes in food, clothing and music, that operate as means of social distinction, with certain practices and commodities considered appropriate for occupants of specific social positions (Bourdieu 1984). Pet ownership is another means to display status, as certain types of pets are indicative of one's social identity or "lifestyle."

Puppy Mills

Producing these animate commodities involves remarkable callousness. Many dogs who are selectively bred and sold for high prices as status symbols suffer serious health problems, such as deformities that prevent them from breathing properly, hip dysplasia, epilepsy, cancer and psychological difficulties. Many dogs sold in pet shops come from puppy mills: factory breeding farms where animals are kept in crowded, filthy conditions. Female dogs are kept in small wire cages, often without room to walk or even urinate properly; many are driven mad by these conditions.

Before 1994, most puppies in Canadian pet shops came from the U.S. but welfare organizations demanded regulations for importing puppies. In 1995, Agriculture Canada required that puppies be at least eight weeks old, microchipped and vaccinated and that their health be checked by a veterinarian. This reduced U.S. imports but provided opportunities for Canadian puppy mills, which are now a major problem. Often located in rural areas and hidden from sight, they create much suffering for animals. A *Winnipeg Free Press* undercover investigation described one such operation: over a hundred dogs, living in soiled straw, drinking green, slimy water, ammonia from urine so strong that it stung the eyes and an overwhelming stench (Hinds 2008). Although Manitoba's chief veterinary officer had an extensive file on operator Dick Wiebe, noting many problems, he still received a licence for his breeding business.

Ontario puppy mills operate with similar deplorable conditions. For example, in September 2007, Linda Taylor of Huron-Kinloss Township was found guilty of confining dogs in an enclosure with inadequate space and failing to provide adequate medical attention. The SPCA removed forty adult dogs and three puppies from her property after finding them with filthy, feces-encrusted fur, living in inadequate conditions, shivering and confined in cages or crates too small for them to fully sit up in.

In Quebec, conditions are even worse because regulations are weak; breeders do not need licences and there are few inspectors. In November 2005, in Blainville, north of Montreal, the SPCA rescued about a hundred dogs living amongst knee-deep piles of excrement, carcasses of dead dogs and a terrible stench that had prompted neighbours' complaints. SPCA Director Pierre Barnoti told CTV News: "There were dead corpses walking. Dogs feeding on dogs, live."

Canada's puppy mills are lucrative businesses. Following the logic of capitalism, which turns all life into commodities, they produce as many puppies as possible, while keeping expenses low; dogs get minimal veterinary care or none at all and poor-quality food and are kept in make-shift cages and sheds. Many are malnourished and sick and are left without water for long periods. As in factory farms, cages are stacked atop each other, allowing excrement to fall onto dogs below, and dead animals are left to decompose. Genetic disorders pass through generations and parvovirus, a highly communicable, frequently fatal disease that affects puppies, is rampant. Many dogs have behaviour problems due to lack of handling and socialization, so they are fearful or aggressive. Breeding females spend their whole lives in small filthy cages. Their only purpose is to produce their quota of puppies. They are bred continuously until they can no longer produce enough puppies to make them profitable, then discarded or killed. Puppy mills sell dogs to pet stores and flea markets or use newspaper advertisements and the Internet. Puppies are taken from their mothers after a few weeks, shipped in crates to pet shops (or research labs), often without food or water, meaning that many die on the trip.

Regulations remain weak. As with anti-cruelty and environmental protection laws, Conservative politicians opposed restrictions on these operations, saying they interfere with people's right to make profits. Again, animals' status as property means their interests are overlooked almost entirely. Hundreds of puppy mills operate in Canada, virtually unregulated, and pet stores still sell dogs from puppy mills. Those wishing to help dogs should adopt them from shelters while supporting laws to eliminate these industries.

Disposable Pets

Although many Canadians love and care for pets, others consider animals disposable. Partly, this reflects disappointments and failures with capitalism's magic system when advertised benefits are contradicted by realities of pet-ownership. Owners may wish to avoid paying medical care, many find responsibilities of caring too time consuming or may wish to replace unfashionable pets with trendier models. In the U.S., six to eight million animals are killed in "shelters" annually. In Canada, humane societies refuse to disclose statistics on animals they kill; Bruce Roney, Ottawa Humane Society executive director says: "We don't talk about the number. It doesn't mean anything" (Denley 2008). Roney says such statistics will be "misused and misrepresented" but acknowledges that "71 per cent of cats and 56 per cent of dogs entering shelters in North America" are killed. The Ontario Humane Society's (OHS) high kill rate and administrative costs prompted a critical movement, Reform the Ottawa Humane Society, to call the OHS "too aggressive" with "euthanasia" and demand an independent review of the organization, more targeted adoptions, fostering programs and rehabilitation programs for animals deemed aggressive. Regardless of specific institutions' policies, the high rate of killing dogs and cats reflects Canadians' readiness to abandon animals and unwillingness to adopt them.

Exotic Pets

The same magical beliefs that facilitate personal identity construction through acquisition of "pure bred" or fierce dogs encourage thousands of Canadians to acquire exotic animals as pets. Owning such animals allows one to express one's identity as "unconventional" or "dangerous." Men, in particular, use aggressive and deadly animals to construct their identity as "outlaws," facilitated by legislation allowing importation of venomous snakes and other exotic animals. Reptiles are a profitable component of the pet business, and are sold in large chain stores, specialty shops and over the Internet at relatively low prices. Ownership is promoted by a growing network of breeders, dealers and hobbyists, all of whom oppose efforts to stop or regulate the trade. Some are captive-bred but many are taken from the wild, where reptiles are threatened not only by the pet trade but also by habitat destruction and hunting. As in the wildlife trade generally, many reptiles die during capture, transit or in captivity when owners cannot care for them properly. Wild animals inhabit complex environments and have needs that cannot be met easily in captivity. While pet stores and dealers promote reptiles as low-maintenance pets requiring little attention, few owners actually can meet their needs. Some keep reptiles in small, barren cages that do not provide room to move, climb or swim. For undomesticated species, captivity can be psychological torture.

In addition to cruelty to animals, keeping exotic pets also endangers native species. In cases where owners no longer want exotic reptiles that are more troublesome than expected and release them into the wild, they can carry diseases that infect local species or, where exotics adapt well to Canadian conditions, they may replace local species, with far-reaching consequences for whole ecosystems (Laidlaw 2005). Despite such serious concerns, when B.C. proposed changing its *Wildlife Act* in 2008 to control importation of alien species in order to protect local ones, the Pet Industry Joint Advisory Council of Canada, representing the industry, opposed such changes, complaining of interference with profits. Individuals assert a right to own exotic animals, disregarding any thought that animals have rights not to be owned or that captivity's negative consequences for them might outweigh their entertainment value for humans.

Keeping exotic species on public display or as pets also creates problems for humans. For example, reptiles are increasingly popular as pets but all carry pathogens that can infect humans. Sometimes, dangers are even more dramatic. In 1992, Larry Moor, founder of the B.C. Association of Reptile Owners, died after being bitten by his Egyptian cobra. Moor was a frequent speaker in schools where he instructed children about reptiles and their handling. Across Canada, several others have been injured or killed by constricting or venomous snakes. In 2006, a Barrie man was bitten after poking his friend's saw-scaled viper. Anti-venom was rushed from Indian River Reptile Zoo in Peterborough, leaving keepers there without supplies and worried for their own safety. In 2007, Jason Hansen watched his finger turn black and his arm swell to four times its normal size after he was bitten by his pet cobra. Hospitals do not store anti-venom to treat such wounds because of costs, the drug's short shelf-life and infrequent need. Although another snake enthusiast supplied his own antidote, doctors at Surrey Memorial Hospital refused to administer it, saying they would not take responsibility because they did not know what it was, that it was too old and that it would be ineffective because the snake had inflicted a "dry" bite, without venom, and that Hansen was suffering from toxins in the snake's saliva. Venomous snakes do not only endanger their keepers. In 2006, Helder Claro's pet cobra escaped in his Toronto home. Residents of a semi-attached rooming house had to evacuate and live elsewhere for months. Assuming that the snake was in the walls, public health officials would not let people enter either building, and area residents feared the snake would appear in their homes. The landlord lost thousands of dollars and property values were threatened. Found guilty of causing a public nuisance, Claro was also charged with sexually assaulting and exploiting teenaged girls at a pet store he had operated. One described how Claro had frightened her by talking about releasing snakes in people's homes. After the snake escaped, authorities found a deadly, insecurely housed Gabon viper in Claro's home, but Claro failed to mention stashing a second cobra in a Tupperware container in his workplace locker; a co-worker who opened the locker narrowly escaped being bitten.

Similar fears arose concerning Dragon Farms in Port Colborne, Ontario, where owner Michael Baran set up a warehouse for his collection of venomous snakes. Located a block from the city hall, the snakes were held in stacked-up aquariums and no anti-venom supplies were available. Baran himself was bitten on one occasion and frantically called for a helicopter to fly him to a treatment centre. A humane society investigation raised concerns about public safety and animal cruelty, but the city said it was unable to contact Baran and refused to trespass into the warehouse.

Some animals carry diseases that threaten human health, and risks are increased by poor conditions. Others may attack their owners when frightened or frustrated, vividly illustrated by the case of Travis, a chimpanzee raised as human, who mauled a Connecticut woman before being shot to death by police in February 2009. Thousands of wild pets need relocation across North America. Large exotic cats, over-bred in private zoos, may be worth more dead and sold for their body-parts than they are alive.

In 2007, the Vancouver Humane Society and the SPCA repeated calls they had been making for years for changes to B.C.'s *Wildlife Act* concerning exotic animals after Tania Dumstey-Soos was killed by a tiger at Siberian Magic, a private zoo owned by her fiancé, extreme fighter and stuntman Kim Carlton, in Bridge Lake, east of 100-Mile

House. She was outside the cage of Gangus, a Bengal tiger, when he lashed out and severed an artery in her leg. She bled to death before an ambulance arrived and, shortly afterwards, Gangus was killed. The SPCA, saying it had grounds for cruelty charges, had spent thousands of dollars trying to have the tigers removed from the zoo, which was described as an accident waiting to happen, with tigers and lions kept in small chain-link cages without flooring. Carlton also walked the tigers, exhibited them at shopping centres, let children feed them and charged visitors to be photographed with them. In 2002, one of Carlton's tigers escaped from a cage in a Fort St. John motel and had to be captured by police.

Suzy, a mixed Bengal-Siberian tiger escaped from Primate Estates, run by Cody and Jamie Bell at Lake Cowichan on Vancouver Island. Police said the tiger was released deliberately; the Bells blamed animal activists trying to discredit what they say is a wildlife sanctuary housing nine other exotic cats, fifty-two primates and assorted reptiles. However, neighbours said several other animals had escaped in the past, causing worries about safety. Bell was forced to remove Suzy, but relocating tigers is difficult. Zoos rejected her because they considered her genetic mix unacceptable for breeding programs. One person offered to buy her, planning to kill her for her pelt and body parts. Bell moved Suzy to the Highlands District home of David Bennett, who spent $15,000 constructing a compound, but anxious neighbours prompted the city to enact a bylaw against owning exotic animals and Bennett was told to remove her. A local business owner founded the Save Suzy Foundation to fund moving her to Colorado's Wildlife Animal Sanctuary, but Bennett opposed this. Amidst arguments about property rights, animal rights and public safety, questions as to whether Bennett "owned" Suzy or had merely "leased" her and competing depictions of Bennett as a hero or as selfish and vain, the controversy illustrates some problems with keeping exotic animals.

Escaped animals are not the only danger. For example, in 1996, David Balac and Jennifer-Ann Cowles were mauled by tigers at

Ontario's drive-through African Lion Safari and Game Park, although their car windows were closed. In 1994, teenager Graydon Edwards was killed by a tiger he considered a pet, after entering a cage containing two tigers and a cougar at his uncle's Walk-A-Bott zoo in Wingham, Ontario; all three animals were killed afterwards.

What is the attraction of keeping dangerous animals such as tigers and venomous snakes? While owners say they keep these animals because they admire and appreciate them, this would be better expressed by helping to preserve those species in their own habitats. Owners acquire exotic pets to augment their self-image; through the same magical processes associated with wearing fur and leather, they imagine that owning a venomous snake or a tiger expresses their own dangerous or wild identity, and, as with hunting, meat-eating, wearing fur, rodeos and so on, dominating animals is typically infused with sexual connotations and emphasis on masculine power. However, keeping such animals is often expensive and difficult. Many quickly tire of the effort and simply discard smaller animals or expect to unload larger ones onto already crowded sanctuaries that are struggling to make ends meet.

Exotic Animals and Zoos

Many enjoy watching exotic animals in zoos, considering this family entertainment. Undoubtedly, parents think zoos develop interest in nature and respect for animals. These are commendable goals but are unlikely to be met by visiting zoos, where children see animals in unnatural surroundings, often forced to perform tricks for food. In such circumstances animals become anthropomorphized clowns, and children learn it is acceptable, even praiseworthy, to imprison them. Aquariums such as Marineland in Niagara Falls are especially striking examples of the cruelty involved in imprisoning large marine mammals such as whales, who normally travel vast distances, in tiny concrete pools. Children are unlikely to learn lessons about compassion at such places, since it is not compassionate to imprison living beings. Although zoos present themselves as educational institutions, it is unclear what we learn about animals there that we cannot learn from reading books or watching films. Any human delight gained by seeing "real animals" is obtained at the expense of their suffering. Few people actually learn anything from visiting zoos. They exist mainly to provide entertainment for humans, and zoo advertising emphasizes "fun."

Animals in zoos are removed from their habitats and placed in cages that prevent natural behaviour. They cannot forage or hunt and have little ability to make choices about their own lives. Many are taken from their families and social groups and kept for years in solitary confinement. For large animals, such as elephants, who naturally live in social groups characterized by rich, complex relationships and who roam over vast distances, it is impossible for zoos to meet their needs. The case of Lucy, an Asian elephant at Edmonton's Valley Zoo, provides a striking example. Lucy is not only kept in a northern country with a harsh climate but in conditions that seem designed to thwart her basic needs. After another elephant, Samantha, was transferred to a North Carolina zoo, Lucy remained isolated in a barren enclosure with little room to roam. Edmonton's climate and the zoo's policy of locking in animals overnight means Lucy spends much of her time inside a barn. Overweight, lethargic and arthritic, she exhibits stereotypic movements common to animals driven mad by captivity. In 2007, after Alaska Zoo agreed to move its lone elephant, Maggie, to PAWS Sanctuary in California, Valley Zoo became the only North American institution keeping an elephant in isolation. Doing so contravenes standards set by the Canadian Association of Zoos and Aquariums and the U.S. Association of Zoos and Aquariums. Although Zoocheck campaigned to move Lucy to a better location at Tennessee's 2,700-acre Elephant Sanctuary, Valley Zoo refused. Their "We Love Lucy" website says Lucy's health conditions prevent moving her and that keepers meet her needs by encouraging her to paint and play musical instruments, activities more likely to amuse humans than satisfy elephants. Despite the usual protestations of "love," it is clear that large charismatic animals constitute key attractions, explaining Valley Zoo's insistence on keeping her imprisoned in such conditions.

Lucy's case is not unique. The SPCA, Vancouver Humane Society and Zoocheck criticized Greater Vancouver Zoo after four hippopotamuses died prematurely. The zoo lost Canadian Association of Zoos and Aquariums certification because of its substandard facilities but went ahead to acquire another hippopotamus, Hazina, who was placed in storage alone in a small concrete building without outdoor access for twenty months while the zoo built a new enclosure. In 2006, the Vancouver Humane Society charged Greater Vancouver Zoo with cruelty for this but the Crown Counsel dropped the charges.

Lickety-Split Ranch and Zoo in London, Ontario, is described by the World Society for the Protection of Animals (WSPA) as Canada's worst zoo. In 2007, Lickety-Split's owner, Shirley McElroy, was charged under the *Fish and Wildlife Conservation Act* with possessing native wildlife without a licence. The WSPA and Zoocheck Canada inspected McElroy's operation and found animals confined in small, barren cages and suffering from health problems. Collapsed buildings and rubbish littered the area. The case drew international attention because of one animal, a Red kangaroo named Tyson. In nature, kangaroos are social animals who can hop up to nine metres in one bound and travel comfortably at 25 kilometres per hour (twice as fast for short distances), but Tyson was kept alone in a small cage that restricted his movement and provided no stimulation. During winter, Tyson's only protection was a tin shed. Australia's *Daily Telegraph* denounced "Kangaroo's Cruel Canada Prison" and encouraged readers to join their "Canada Kicking Page," which featured a video of comedians Robin Williams singing "Blame Canada" and Weird Al Yankovic performing "Canadian Idiot" (Howden and Campion 2007). (The outcry illustrates both the use of animals as symbols of national identity and the moral schizophrenia of a society that kills millions of animals for food while protesting mistreatment of a single animal of a different species. Furthermore, Australians' own attitudes towards kangaroos are mixed: in 2002, Australia's government raised the number of kangaroos to be killed commercially from 5.5 million to 7 million, drawing cheers from farmers and the multi-million-dollar kangaroo meat and skin industry. Of course, such hypocrisy does not change the fact that Tyson suffered from confinement in Canada.)

At her court appearance, described by local media as "a circus," McElroy brandished a Bible and cited supernatural justifications for domination over animals, rejecting the court's interference with her "God-given right." Unable to silence her, Justice of the Peace Helen Gale left the courtroom until her rant ended. However, by the time McElroy went to court, Tyson had disappeared. McElroy refused to reveal his fate. He may have been sold or died and been buried in a secret location. McElroy missed a later court appearance and failed to renew her annual zoo licence in 2007. In August 2008, the London Humane Society, Ontario's Ministry of Natural Resources and police entered Lickety-Split Ranch to rescue native species but under provincial law were powerless to remove exotic animals. In September 2008, London's environment and transportation committee described Lickety-Split as an embarrassment to the city and recommended repealing McElroy's licence. Although Zoocheck, WSPA and other groups had campaigned against roadside zoos in Canada for many years, it was only in 2008 that Ontario agreed to new legislation.

Unknown numbers of exotic animals are kept as pets and in roadside zoos. In 1997, the Ontario Humane Society estimated there were five hundred exotic cats in that province alone. Canada's exotic pet trade is part of a global multi-billion-dollar wildlife trade comparable in value to illegal weapons trading. It includes use of animals as food, as medicine, as research tools, for their skins, fur, feathers, horns and shells and as trophies for sport hunters. Breeders, dealers, auctions, legal and illegal imports, online sales and roadside zoos are all aspects of Canada's exotic animal and wildlife trade. Mount Forest, Ontario, holds the Fur and Feather Swap, specializing in exotic birds. One of Canada's largest auctions is Innisfail's Odd and Exotic Animal Sale, which has been held for decades around Thanksgiving and Easter. Ontario's Livestock Exchange in Waterloo hosts the Tiger Paw Exotics Sale, where one can obtain camels, zebras and llamas. Rob Laidlaw, director of Zoocheck Canada, describes tigers sold in Ontario for $100, saying "Lions and tigers are a dime a dozen, there are so many around" (Taylor 2007).

There is little good to say about zoos and many reasons to close them. In some situations, habitat destruction is advancing so rapidly that some form of captivity may be the only hope of survival for certain species, such as orangutans in Borneo and Sumatra, where palm oil plantations are replacing rainforests. Orangutans likely will be extinct in the wild within a decade; either they will disappear entirely or a few survivors will be maintained in artificial environments, but preferably this should mean sanctuaries, where they will not be on public display. While zoos emphasize their role in conservation and breeding animals, few actually breed endangered animals and, even in the case of those that do, these programs take place outside the zoo itself, indicating there is no need for animal displays at all.

8. PETS OR MEAT?

Confusions within Speciesist Ideology

Our anthropocentric, speciesist ideas about animals determine their treatment. We classify certain animals as pets and lucky pets receive affection and good treatment (although some are not so lucky and become targets of abuse). Canadians classify mainly dogs and cats as pets, but the category has broadened to include guinea pigs, birds, ferrets and reptiles. Other, less lucky animals are classified as food: their fate is grim. These confused and incoherent ways of thinking about and treating animals constitute "moral schizophrenia" (Francione 2000).

Some animals occupy a position between these categories. For example, some rabbits live as pets in our homes; others are crammed into filthy wire cages until they are killed for their fur or flesh. Rabbits raised as livestock in Canada do not receive even the pretence of protection given to other animals under industrial codes of practice and can be slaughtered while fully conscious after enduring a lifetime of suffering. Agriculture Canada noted 2,747 rabbit farms in Canada in 2006 and recorded a federal and provincial slaughter of 599,635, although an unknown number were killed by do-it-yourself methods. Statistics Canada does not appear to keep records of rabbits killed for fur.

Horses also occupy this in-between position — some people eat horses, but others are disturbed by this because they classify horses as companion animals or sport animals, worthy of concern, although their inconsistent ideas and ethics readily accept consumption of other types of animals. In December 2008, residents of McBride, B.C., abandoned Christmas preparations but gained international media coverage and applause after a week digging through deep snow to rescue two emaciated horses abandoned to almost-certain death by their owner. Edmonton lawyer Frank Mackay, who did not help with digging, tried to reclaim the horses but was charged with cruelty. Meanwhile, the B.C. SPCA was considering cruelty charges in the case of starving horses found on the Canim Lake First Nations reserve. Although the emaciated animals were in plain sight of the main village, no one provided them with food. Although turning out horses in winter to fend for themselves is common practice throughout B.C., outrage was directed against the Canim band as well as towards the SPCA because it only responded after the case received national media coverage (Wingrove 2009).

Canadian Opportunism

After a public campaign to end the horse-slaughter industry, the last U.S. horse-slaughter plant closed in 2007. However, legislation did not prohibit transporting horses for slaughter elsewhere, immediately increasing numbers shipped to Canada and Mexico. While consumption of horses is rare in the U.S. and horse slaughterhouses have closed there, Canada observes no such scruples; every year many thousands of live horses are imported to be killed at seven federally licensed slaughterhouses. Canadians themselves do not eat much horseflesh; a 2004 Ipsos Reid poll found 64 percent of Canadians opposed slaughter of horses for human consumption. However, industries tirelessly campaign to overcome compassionate feelings about horses and to relegate them to the status of "food animals," using celebrity "foodies" who increasingly touted horse flesh as a gourmet product. Chef Gordon Ramsay declared it tasty and nutritious, urging diners to eat it (Harrison 2007). Clarissa Dickson

Wright, another television chef, on *Two Fat Ladies*, also endorsed horse flesh. In *Time* magazine, Joel Stein (2007) pronounced horse flesh "awesome," untroubled by his own acknowledgement that it is cruel to kill horses (and that it is "equally bad" to kill other animals). Gourmets ignore moral questions about horse flesh, and restaurants and butcher shops willingly supply it. In *Toronto Life* (McBride 2007), Jason McBride praised one restaurant's cedar-pressed horsemeat tapas as "perfect for sharing" as a Mother's Day treat, and Robert Fulford defended horsemeat consumption in the *Financial Post* (Fulford 2008). These efforts to shift conceptual boundaries for horses exemplify how marketing strategies socialize consumers and train them to distance animals and transform them into objects of consumption, minimizing emotional bonds and ethical responsibilities and discouraging any sense of justice towards animals. Of course, from an animal rights perspective this sense of justice should be expanded to include all animals, not just those we happen to have designated as "pets." In this sense, industry has been more consistent in its readiness to exploit all animals, if profits can be made. The Canadian government, too, has avoided moral schizophrenia, exemplified by its opposition to banning importation of cat and dog fur in defence of Canada's sealing industry, and in its willingness to support the horsemeat industry.

Canada's Horse-Killing Industry

Canada is among the world's largest producers of horsemeat: 13,701 tons in 2007, worth tens of millions of dollars ($74 million in 1998). In 2008, horse imports from the U.S. rose sharply and the 79,613 horses killed in federally and provincially inspected slaughterhouses in 2007 was over 50 percent more than the previous year's total of 50,067. In 2008, 112,887 horses were slaughtered in Canada; exports grow every year.

Horses sent to slaughter include workhorses who are considered no longer useful, show jumpers who can no longer perform, older horses from riding-stables, those no longer wanted at racetracks and horses rejected by the pregnant mare urine industry. Those not destined for human consumption are made into other products such as pet food, fertilizer or glue. Flesh of horses killed in Canada is mainly exported to France, Japan and Italy. Canada also exports live horses to Japan so gourmets there can purchase their flesh freshly killed. Canada previously exported live horses to the U.S. for slaughter although in 2006, the House of Representatives passed a bill to ban killing horses for meat. However, the U.S. Senate did not move on the *American Horse Slaughter Prevention Act* before the Congressional session ended. In 2008, H.R. Bill 6598, the *Prevention of Equine Cruelty Act*, was introduced to the U.S. House of Representatives and passed by the Judiciary Committee but Congress delayed passage. The same Act (now H.R. 503) was reintroduced in the U.S. House on January 14, 2009, with the aim of prohibiting sale or export of horses for slaughter.

Horses arrive at slaughterhouses from auctions and stockyards, where they are held and transported in atrocious conditions and sold for pennies per pound, translating into huge profits when their flesh is sold abroad. Agriculture Canada and the CFIA defend the industry, describing killing as humane. Emaciated, injured and sick, horses arrive at the slaughterhouse and are tightly crowded into pens, then channelled into killing chutes, where a captive-bolt pistol fires a heavy steel rod into their heads. Death is supposedly instantaneous, but horses struggle to escape and many are shot numerous times before being killed. Although veterinarians working for the CFIA are supposed to examine horses at slaughterhouses, undercover investigations show they are often absent and, in any event, their concern is with the condition of food for human consumption, not the animals' well-being.

Many horses sent to slaughterhouses are rejects from the hugely profitable racing industry, with expenditures worth over $2 billion a year in Ontario alone, with betting totaling $1.73 billion in Canada in 2005, mainly in Ontario, followed by $213 million in British

Columbia and $159 million in Alberta, although these figures reflect a decline from previous years due to expansion of illegal foreign Internet gambling. Horses used in racing are selectively bred, which creates health problems for them. They are transported from track to track, where they are forced to run at top speed, whipped by human riders, and they suffer tendon and muscles injuries, fractures, broken legs and heart attacks. To keep them in the race, horses are given various drugs, anti-inflammatories, painkillers and steroids, some legal and others not. Even though they may have cost millions of dollars and earned millions more for their owners, few race-horses are rewarded with comfortable retirement in a pasture. Maintaining such large animals is costly; many owners are unwilling to pay so their horses are "repurposed" and sold for slaughter. This includes famous race horses such as Ferdinand, son of Canadian-bred Nijinsky II, who won the 1986 Kentucky Derby; he died in a Japanese slaughterhouse after breeders determined he had outlived his value as a stallion. The American Society for the Prevention of Cruelty to Animals estimates that 10 percent of North America's race horses are sent to slaughter. At Cookstown Stockyards, north of Toronto, over 30 percent of horses auctioned for slaughter are racehorses (Morrison 2008). During transport to slaughter, they suffer the same cruelties that other "food animals" endure: overcrowding, injuries, extreme temperatures and lack of food and water, followed by terror and pain as they are killed.

The racing industry has little compassion or concern for horses. Trainer Emile Corbel sold Good Luck Peter to slaughter when she failed to perform well at Winnipeg's Assiniboia Downs Racetrack, expressing only contempt for her:

> It was a Manitoba-bred, really small, looked like a new breed of sheep. She couldn't run, was ugly and stupid. So we killed her. What else can you do? If you buy a rat, especially a Manitoba rat, you can't give it away. Then you have to kill them. (Wiecek 2006)

Others who profit from slaughtering horses present themselves as defenders of those animals, concerned about their welfare. On CBC Radio's (2006) *The Current*, Dr. Terry Whiting, chair of the Canadian Veterinary Medical Association's Animal Welfare Committee, opposed banning horse slaughter because it might lead to more neglect. The American Veterinary Medical Association used the same argument against proposed U.S. legislation to ban horse slaughter. Clearly, if one is concerned about abuse of horses (or any other animals), the sensible course is to devote greater efforts towards protection and prevention and to ensuring that abuse does not occur, rather than murdering potential victims.

Whiting distinguished horses from "companion animals," claiming that slaughtering horses is acceptable if done "humanely." Slaughterhouses do not kill animals humanely; the process is nothing like euthanasia for those who are terminally ill and suffering. Commercial slaughter is a business undertaken for profit, not an act of mercy. Whiting says slaughter is "humane" because veterinarians are present. Yet these veterinarians work for the industry. The Canadian Horse Defence Coalition (CHDC) notes that Whiting himself is employed by Manitoba's Ministry of Agriculture and argues that, due to obvious conflicts of interest, veterinarians on animal welfare committees should have no ties to food production. Having veterinarians working in slaughterhouses seems as bizarre as physicians' participation in the Nazis' efforts to exterminate Jews and other "undesirable" populations. No doubt, veterinarians who assist in slaughtering animals duplicate processes of psychic numbing that Lifton (2000) describes among the Nazi doctors. While it seems odd that veterinarians (who we think should care for animals) oppose efforts to protect them, many are unconcerned with welfare (let alone rights) of animals but see themselves as technicians who assist with management of animals owned as property.

Success of horse advocates in the U.S. allowed Canadians to cash in on slaughter. Eager to profit from Canada's failure to protect horses, slaughterhouse operators here increased business as

U.S. companies began shipping horses across the border. Industry representatives were ecstatic. Commenting on tens of thousands of horses killed in Alberta slaughterhouses, Les Burwash, Manager of Horse Programs, Alberta Agriculture & Rural Development, said: "We're happy to have a slaughter plant in Alberta. It's a viable way to create a value for all horses." According to Troutman (2008), "Burwash says that if Alberta did not have a horse slaughter industry, a significant portion of horses would have no or negative value." Anthropocentric logic concludes that animals have no value unless humans can profit from them in some way, including their death.

Cruelty and Killing

In June 2008, the CHDC released video footage, shown on CBC's *The National* news, depicting cruel treatment of horses slaughtered at Natural Valley Farms in Neudorf, Saskatchewan. Natural Valley had received a multi-million-dollar government grant to expand cow-killing operations. However, Natural Valley is affiliated with U.S.-based Cavel International and its Belgian parent corporation, Velda, which owned the last U.S. horse slaughterhouse to close in 2007, in DeKalb, Illinois. Notorious for violations of U.S. law, Cavel engineered what industrial consultant and horse advocate John Holland (2007) called "a brazen coup" in getting "the Canadian government and cattle producers… to pay for the construction of a plant to help the beef producers, when at least part of its purpose will be for horse slaughter." Ken Piller, president of Natural Valley Farms explained the industry's cruel calculations: "We saw an opportunity here…. Nobody in Saskatchewan cares. Everybody here raises horses…. Everybody understands at the end of the day there has to be a cull" (Harding 2007).

Violations of even those minimal standards that do exist in Canada appeared immediately. In 2007, Animals' Angels Canada investigated Natural Valley and found a pit where remains of cows and horses were dumped. They found heads of horses who had been butchered but saw no captive-bolt-pistol holes and questioned how they were killed. The CHDC documented violations of Canadian food inspection laws, including transport of animals on double-decker trailers, transport of horses wearing horseshoes, failure to protectively separate horses during transport, transport of sick, injured, blind and emaciated horses, transport of pregnant horses, cross-border transport of horses and unsupervised nighttime unloading, failure to provide food or water to horses penned overnight, overcrowding, horses slipping and rearing in fright in killing pens, a worker beating a horse with a stick, improper stunning before slaughter, with approximately 30 percent of the horses being slaughtered while fully conscious, and discovery of a full-term foal thrown in a rendering pit. Although a CFIA veterinarian was posted at the plant, there was no effort to stop abuses. Twyla Francois from the CHDC said that in twelve hours of footage she reviewed no CFIA inspector was present at the kill pen, in violation of government regulations requiring an agency veterinarian be present to monitor slaughter operations.

The CHDC demanded immediate closure of the Natural Valley killing plant and a complete ban on slaughter of horses for human consumption. Instead of complying, government and industry groups rallied to defend Natural Valley and slaughtering practices generally. Although the plant clearly violated government regulations, federal Agriculture Minister Gerry Ritz defended its operations and the CFIA praised the plant. The day after the CBC ran the footage, Scott Brown, from Saskatchewan's Agriculture Department, told CBC News (2008b): "The provincial government supports the humane slaughter of animals," although he acknowledged that the horrifying video raised "some concerns." Shanyn Silinski, executive director of the Manitoba Farm Animal Council, an industry lobby group, said slaughter was regulated, dismissed the video footage and argued that slaughter should be "done properly, not banned." Like many industry lobbyists, she presented killing animals for profit as humane efforts to prevent their suffering: "Do we want to be in a situation like the U.S. where they're turning them loose in public lands to have them starve to death or be killed by predators?" No other alternative, such as establishing and supporting sanctuaries or encouraging adoption of horses, occurs to industry defenders.

The industry mobilized to form the Horse Welfare Alliance of Canada (HWAC). In true Orwellian fashion, this consists of government agencies and corporations based upon animal exploitation. In fact, many organizations claiming to represent "welfare" of animals exist to defend exploitation, including slaughter. In this case, the alliance includes provincial equestrian associations and farm animal councils, along with Agriculture and Agri-Food Canada, the CFIA, North American Equine Ranching Information Council (a lobby group promoting the pregnant mare urine industry), J. Woods Livestock Services and two horsemeat producers, Bouvry Exports of Calgary (Canada's largest exporter of horsemeat) and Natural Valley Farms itself.

Saskatchewan's Society for the Prevention of Cruelty to Animals seems to have considered these exploiters of animals congenial partners. The HWAC website notes the economic value of horses and touts horsemeat but devotes little attention to actual well-being of horses. Individual HWAC members also defended horse slaughter at Natural Valley Farms. For example, in the October 2008 edition of its quarterly *Whoa!* newsletter, the Ontario Equestrian Foundation presented its version of "The Truth about Horse Slaughter in Canada." Vice-president Gary Yaghdjan describes his CFIA-guided tour of Natural Valley Farms, praises the "compassion" of the "highly trained" killers who "provid[e] these animals dignity by using the best welfare practices available" and lauds commercial slaughter as a humane method of dealing with unwanted horses. Again, no other option is discussed or even recognized.

Despite receiving millions in federal and provincial government funding, Natural Valley Farms defaulted on a loan and went into receivership in September 2008. Nevertheless, Velda corporation ensured that killing continued, taking over as the Natural Meat Company. Despite government assurances of "humane" practices, there is no reason to expect that conditions improved under Velda's management.

Natural Valley portrayed abuses as aberrations. However, Animals' Angels (2007) revealed similar conditions at another horse-slaughter plant, Richelieu Meats in Massueville, Quebec. Again, no veterinarian was present during unloading, and workers used electric prods to move the horses, who were in poor condition, emaciated, suffering tumours and broken limbs. In holding-pens, horses had no water or food or shelter from inclement weather. Conditions were filthy. Horses were observed "shaking in terror" in a killing pen smeared with blood and remains of other horses. When questioned about dead horses in the parking lot, Richelieu's Francois Bouvry explained they were "too lazy to walk to the water trough." One worker was observed feigning sexual intercourse with a dead horse, encouraged by his fellow workers' laughter. Existence of such institutionalized forms of cruelty generates individual cruelty, desensitizing humans and allowing them to be as vulgar and debased as can be imagined.

Premarin

Many horses are slaughtered as byproducts of Canada's Premarin industry. Premarin (also marketed as Prempro, Premphase and Prempac) is an estrogen drug derived from pregnant mares' urine (PMU) and is the only estrogen-replacement therapy derived from animals. It is given to menopausal women to prevent hot flashes and ease symptoms of menopause. Marketed since the 1940s, by the end of the twentieth century it had become one of the world's most-prescribed drugs, taken by millions of women and worth billions of dollars. However, in 1999 profits plummeted and the industry tottered as serious health risks became widely known.

The industry is dominated by one producer, Ayerst Organics, a subsidiary of Philadelphia's Wyeth pharmaceuticals, based in Montreal, but operating from Brandon, Manitoba. Premarin became

Canada's biggest pharmaceutical export, and Brandon became known as the "world's capital of pregnant mare's urine" and also for the waste from Ayerst's operation, which was overwhelming the city's sewage system.

To maintain a supply of estrogen-saturated urine, tens of thousands of mares are kept constantly pregnant, artificially impregnated, sometimes only days after giving birth and separated immediately from their foals. The foals are unnecessary byproducts, and thousands are sold to slaughterhouses. Confined in small stalls, many horses cannot lie down and are not exercised for months on end; many are kept in the same position for months and tied up for most of the year (their pregnancies last eleven months). On some PMU operations, one worker may control a hundred horses, meaning that they receive little individual attention. Each horse is strapped to a urine-collection bag and the liquid is drained through hoses into plastic jugs outside their stalls. Farmers collect the jugs and ship them to Ayerst.

Investigations by the WSPA found substandard conditions, dead horses, untreated wounds, illnesses, overcrowding, restrictions on movement and restricted access to water so that the urine is more concentrated (a tactic that causes dehydration as well as liver and renal problems for the horses).

Although horses normally live twenty to thirty years, many in the Premarin industry are scrapped after ten. Like their disposable babies who have preceded them, when mares can no longer become pregnant, they are sent to slaughterhouses; those considered unsatisfactory for human consumption are turned into pet food. Callous treatment typifies Canadian auctions:

> One of the saddest things I ever saw was an old, used-up Belgium mare being sold for meat at one of the auctions. She had a cheap halter on that was embedded in her head. Her owner wanted the halter back after she was sold to the killers so he ripped it off and she had this gaping hole in her head. She stood there shaking and bleeding profusely and

nobody did anything to help her. (Equine Advocates n.d.)

Although corporate propaganda trumpets industry's concern for animal welfare, no concern or compassion is in evidence as those involved defend their brutality, often in violent and thuggish ways. When *Globe and Mail* reporter Katherine Harding (2007) asked Pat Houde, licensed agent for Calgary's Bouvry Exports and a former rodeo bull-rider, elk-farmer and feedlot owner in Elm Creek, near Winnipeg, about his notoriety as one of Canada's main buyers of horses for slaughter, he responded: "I don't want to say a fucking thing." But he had been more forthcoming previously on the Premarin industry, in describing his treatment of mares and foals: "We crush 'em and recycle 'em… just like aluminum cans" (SPCA of Monterey County 1999). In 1998, Houde was charged with assaulting a Project Equus crew filming a documentary on Premarin from the road outside his feedlot. Houde ran them into a ditch with his truck, beat them and tried to take their camera. Two crew members required hospital treatment. In 2001, Houde threatened a *Vancouver Sun* reporter covering meat buyers at a Winnipeg horse auction (Morrison 2008).

While deriving huge profits from exploitation of horses, Ayerst consistently denied responsibility for their mistreatment, blaming farmer contractors who run their operations. Yet, according to animal protection group United Animal Nations, Wyeth even prevented contracted farmers from cooperating with rescue groups willing to provide homes for unwanted foals because the corporation believed this might damage their image and raise questions about cruelty to animals.

Exploiters defend cruelty as necessary to meet human needs but even this self-serving defence is false. It is unnecessary to subject horses to this cruelty; at least a dozen other available drugs do the same thing as Premarin. Synthetic forms of the drug have been available for years so cruelty is not necessary to help women avoid these symptoms. Premarin is also very expensive. Although a generic form exists, Wyeth was able to keep it off the market because it is not absorbed in women's bodies at exactly the same rate.

It is ironic that Premarin — an animal-derived product — is used to treat problematic symptoms of menopause, which are themselves intensified by consumption of other animal products. For example, in Japan, menopause is much less of a problem for women; few report hot flashes and other bothersome symptoms. Japanese women eat a healthier diet consisting of less meat, less animal fat, more soy products and more fibre. North American women eat much more meat and about four times as much fat as Japanese women. Consequently, they have far higher levels of estrogen and more problems with menopause. Japanese women have lower estrogen levels before and after menopause, so symptoms of menopause are very mild or nonexistent. (Japanese women also have lower rates of osteoporosis and heart disease.) Also, North American women with vegetarian, low-fat diets have fewer problems. Thus, adopting a healthier vegetarian diet would improve the lives of both humans and animals. Furthermore, estrogen derived from horse urine is linked to breast and endometrial cancer, higher blood pressure, gallstones and osteoporosis. Other side effects include bleeding, blood clots, cramping, headaches and yeast infections. Thus, Premarin is expensive, possibly dangerous to human health and responsible for unnecessary suffering of animals, while alternatives are available.

The PMU industry peaked around the turn of the twenty-first century and is now faltering. Numbers of PMU farms decreased sharply, and in 2003 and 2005 Wyeth dropped contracts with many ranchers, leaving them with thousands of pregnant mares and unwanted foals. Unprepared for other careers, some ranchers continue breeding horses and selling foals to slaughter. Canada's PMU industry should be ended sooner rather than later, and rescue groups should be supported in their efforts to adopt horses to good homes where they can be properly cared for and loved.

Contradictions in Animal Protection

Many who oppose slaughtering horses consider it acceptable kill cows or pigs and do not object to using horses in rodeos or racing. They are not animal rights supporters or vegetarians, but feel special attachment to horses as others do for dogs or cats and do not want them to be eaten. Moral schizophrenia also surfaces among groups that protect only certain animals. The *National Post* (Vallis 2008) quotes Shelley Grainger of the CHDC: "They're companion animals, they're support animals, they go to the Olympics. Policemen ride them to protect us…. They're a symbol of nobility and so many other things that livestock just aren't." Of course, the fact that horses are symbols of nobility and other animals (who are only identified as "livestock") "just aren't" is a social construction that reflects the economics of the industries that exploit these animals. In other societies, cows, for example, are, indeed, considered noble animals.

Similarly, the now-defunct Toronto-based Help Horses (n.d.) group formed to help horses threatened with slaughter due to drought conditions in Alberta. Its website poses and answers the question: "We kill cows and pigs — what's the difference with horses?"

> Cows, pigs, chicken and other "livestock" are raised for food. They are bred specially for this purpose as well as fed certain feed and given certain drugs that are not supposed to be harmful to humans when their meat is consumed.
>
> Horses on the other hand are raised as our companions, they come from a variety of places where they are fed, medicated and treated differently. From family pets that could no longer be afforded to premarin foals, horses are not monitored before they are slaughtered as other animals are.
>
> In our society horses are companion animals. It is evident in the way we treat horses. Dog and cat shows are similar to horse shows where the animal is not only judged by its looks, but by the way they can perform. Horses and

dogs have long been members of the Canadian police force, unlike any other animal. You decide? Would you eat Trigger, or Mr. Ed or Silver? It would be like eating Benji or Lassie to most Canadians.

As Help Horses says, Canadians are horrified at the idea of eating dogs (although some cultures accept this) so, because horses are closer to dogs in our system of classifying animals, we should not eat them. But this raises other questions: why do we consider it acceptable to eat a cow? Help Horses merely expresses a tautology, that it is acceptable to eat these other animals because we eat them. Contradictions in how we see animals — as pets or meat — are obvious to children. For example, in 2002, two young girls from Cupids, Newfoundland, Katie Harvey (then ten) and sister Emma (then seven) created SaveAlbertaHorses.com to raise money for horses who were being sold to slaughterhouses due to severe drought and lack of feed. Their efforts saved 104 horses and one donkey. They explained their motivation:

Why We Love Horses
I love horses because they are really cute. I am always in the mood to go and visit horses. I don't have a horse of my own but I hope someday to get one! I also like horses because you can ride them and I really like the feeling of riding. I like the sounds they make too. One thing I really like about horses is their mane, you could put the horses hair up any way you want. My favorite colour horse is white, but I don't know why. I find horses have a really sweet personality, that is another thing I like about them. Horses are really fantastic, that is why I chose to save them. —Katie Harvey

I love horses because they are pretty and they are cute. I like horses because I can ride them and they are nice. —Emma Harvey

The girls added a manifesto indicating that even children can see through the moral schizophrenia involved in treating some animals as pets and others as food:

> If We Ran the World
> 1.   Everyone would have at least one horse.
> 2.   Everyone would be a vegetarian.
> 3.   No slaughtering any animals.
> 4.   There would be no poor people.
> 5.   Everyone would have everlasting money.
> 6.   No bad people or terrorists.
> 7.   Everyone was friends with everyone else.
> 8.   Everyone will be able to have riding lessons for free.
> 9.   Almost everyone would be farmers because we all have to have vegetables if we're all vegetarians

Although expressed in childish terms and still endorsing the idea of animals as property and use of animals for human ends, the girls' thinking seems more ethically consistent than that of groups that oppose killing some animals while accepting slaughter of others. An animal rights perspective urges us to see beyond the social construction of some animals as pets and others as meat and to consider all animals' interests equally.

9. VIVISECTION

Blank Cheques for Torture and Killing

"Vivisection" describes animal testing in general; it denotes the unbearable suffering and death of millions of animals every year in North American laboratories, run by private corporations and public universities. Vivisection is a booming industry in Canada. Breeders, dealers and researchers, as well as companies that manufacture food, cages, tools and instruments all have vested interests in continuing animal experimentation and avoiding development of alternatives. Vivisectors, criticized throughout history for their cruelties, understand it is best to operate in secret, blocking access, withholding information and deploying misleading euphemisms. Just as Canada's factory farms and slaughterhouses operate behind locked gates and sealers attempt to evade observation through the misleadingly named Seal Protection Regulations, Canada's vivisection industry has arranged to exempt itself from public scrutiny. The Canadian Council on Animal Care (CCAC) is the national body that oversees animal use in research. It was formed in 1968 by vivisectors and is dominated by those with direct interests in continuing these practices. Compliance with CCAC inspections is entirely voluntary, and private laboratories are not subject to any inspection whatsoever. Inspections are announced in advance, conducted when institutions agree and done by other vivisectors; all reports are confidential, no sanctions have ever been imposed.

Rather than undertaking critical initiatives to promote animal welfare, as its name misleadingly suggests, the CCAC, instead, advocates for researchers. For example, in hearings before the Standing Committee on Justice and Human Rights concerning much-needed modification of Canada's antiquated and ineffective anti-cruelty legislation, the CCAC opposed changes and demanded specific exemptions for animal research, despite the fact that Canadian laws already provide this. Essentially, the CCAC is a means by which vivisectors evade regulation.

For example, Jim Pfaus, neuroscience professor at Concordia University in Montreal, used rats to develop his drug PT-141 to enhance female sexual arousal. The *Montreal Gazette* (2007) says Pfaus "makes sure he and his students carefully follow guidelines for humane use of the rats and their euthanasia — protocols issued by the Canadian Council on Animal Care." However, Pfaus is an ethics reviewer for the CCAC and is unlikely to impose standards that would impede his own research. Michael O'Sullivan, executive director of the Humane Society of Canada, says the CCAC is dominated by vivisection groups: "All they do is scratch each other's backs so they can get the funding they need to continue their projects" (quoted in *Montreal Gazette* 2007).

Sztybel (n.d.) argues that the CCAC's code of ethics provides at least four "blank cheques" to vivisectors. First, the CCAC's ethics guidelines allow an extensive list of painful procedures that can be inflicted on animals (in fact, nothing is prohibited) as long as an external review is conducted. However, that review will be conducted by other vivisectors who not only have conflicts of interest but have been desensitized to regard animals only as "experimental models." Second, vivisection is deemed acceptable if it has a "reasonable expectation" of contributing to knowledge. But this restriction is meaningless since any detail, no matter how trivial, can be said to add to knowledge. Third, the code permits researchers to use animals as long as they have made an effort to find alternatives, a recommendation that is unenforceable and regularly violated. The final blank cheque is the voluntary nature of the CCAC guidelines, and private testing industries have no obligation to pay the CCAC to inspect their facilities. Sztybel concludes that the CCAC's code may actually be worse than having none at all because it "give[s] the illusion of protection to animals when it really just helps to facilitate their death and degradation in Canadian laboratories."

Inspections are done once every three to five years, laboratories receive advance warning and confidentiality agreements prevent inspectors from discussing anything they see. In a 2003 interview with CBC television's *Disclosure* program, CCAC's executive director Dr. Clement Gauthier acknowledged that in what then had been thirty-four years of operation, the CCAC had not stopped a single experiment. The CBC found "little transparency" in the CCAC and the entire vivisection industry but noted that "more animals are being subjected to higher levels of pain in lab experiments" and that Canada's lack of federal laws on animal research could make it a haven for experimenters whose activities are banned elsewhere. Determined to protect vivisectors' interests rather than those of animals, the CCAC joined other animal-exploitation industries to oppose updating Canada's outdated anti-cruelty laws. Although Gauthier stated on-camera that his group was not lobbying against anti-cruelty legislation, the CBC exposed this as a lie, showing the CCAC's position statement opposing legislation and Gauthier's own letter urging CCAC members to write to government expressing concerns about proposed legislation. The CCAC is simply a front group for the vivisection industry, providing a veneer of legitimacy while ensuring that researchers can conduct their activities in secret, free from interference from the public who fund them.

The CCAC reports that vivisection in Canada increased steadily over the past decade. Over two and a half million animals were used in 2006, compared to less than one and a half million in 1997. Mainly, researchers use rats, mice and fish, but thousands of other animals including sheep, pigs, rabbits, cats, dogs and non-human primates are considered research tools. The CCAC divides experiments into four "Categories of Invasiveness," ranging from "little or no discomfort or stress" to "severe pain near, at, or above the pain tolerance threshold of unanaesthetized conscious animals." Numbers of animals used in this most invasive category tripled over the last decade.

Canadian universities recognize that vivisection means money. The University of Guelph trademarked its EnviroPig, a transgenic animal designed to produce lower-phosphorus less-polluting manure, although effects of consuming the flesh of transgenic animals are unknown. The University of British Columbia considers itself a leader in biomedical research, operating a large rodent-breeding centre and thirty animal facilities, and, fuelled by lucrative grants, plans to expand with a new medical centre and increased staff. UBC's misnamed Animal Care Center (ACC) provides 100,000 animals each year for university-affiliated research. However, questioned about successes achieved by animal research at UBC, Dr. Chris Harvey-Clark, director of the ACC, was unable to name a single example (*Ubyssey* 2008).

Unproven Claims

Vivisectors make extreme, but unproven, claims about animal testing. Matthews (2008) notes that academics and institutions such as the Royal Society, the U.K. Department of Health and the U.S. Department of Health endorsed the statement that "virtually every medical achievement of the last century has depended directly or indirectly on research with animals." Yet Matthews finds that this statement is unverified by data and is merely an assertion that says nothing about the inferential value of animal research. If animal experiments are ubiquitous, it is unsurprising that they were involved in medical achievements, but that does not mean the achievements depended upon animal experiments. Matthews notes that since animal testing is mandatory, crediting these tests as the source of the breakthrough makes as much sense as attributing it to wearing lab coats. One could just as well attribute every medical failure of the last century to animal research. Indeed, opponents of vivisection cite many cases in which animal experiments delayed development of drugs that are helpful to humans and cases in which drugs that are harmful or even lethal to humans were approved and marketed because animal testing suggested they were safe.

There is a "striking paucity" of quantitative data showing the value of animal models for human health, and in those rare instances where reviews of the predictive value of animal models do exist, important data are lacking, so "it is simply impossible to assess the evidential weight provided by the animal models" and "the data provide no statistically credible evidence that these animal models contribute any predictive value" (Matthews 2008: 96–97).

Although testing on mice provided data on basic immunological mechanisms, Mark M. Davis (2008), of the Department of Microbiology and Immunology at Stanford University's School of Medicine, warns of overreliance on mouse models, saying "mice are lousy models for clinical studies," and notes disappointing results from mouse models in cancer immunotherapy and neurological diseases. Noting the "sheer evolutionary distance" and substantial physiological differences between mice and humans, Davis concludes we are in "a state of denial where there is so much invested in the mouse model that it seems almost unthinkable to look elsewhere" despite the fact that more relevant information can be gained through new developments such as the Human Genome Project and broader, industrial-scale studies on data that can be collected from human subjects. Davis recommends more sophisticated infrastructure for processing large-scale data and meta-analysis of existing literature.

Animal testing has not prevented adverse human reactions. Frequently, drugs continue to human trials even where animal tests showed harmful effects, as in the case of nimodipine, considered a potential treatment for stroke victims. Commercial pressure pushes pharmaceutical corporations to continue development even where animal testing suggests danger. In other cases, animal testing suggested drugs were safe but effects on humans have been disastrous. There is an extensive record of misleading information obtained from animal research. For example, the antibiotic chloramphenicol was withdrawn after producing fatal anemia in humans despite extensive testing on animals that showed no ill effects. The anti-inflammatory opren killed at least sixty-one people from liver damage although toxicity tests on monkeys (involving far higher doses) indicated no danger. Thousands of asthmatics died after taking isoprenaline through inhalers yet animal tests showed the drug to be safe. Heart-disease drug practolol passed animal tests but blinded many humans. Cough suppressant zipeprol was deemed safe after animal testing but resulted in seizures and comas in humans. The most well-known case is thalidomide, developed by German pharmaceutical company Grunenthal and sold world-wide from 1957 to 1961 to counteract nausea in pregnant women. Although testing on rats and mice showed no adverse effects, the drug caused birth defects in approximately 10,000 humans. Although tested on animals, Merck corporation's drug Vioxx caused between 88,000 and 139,000 heart attacks, 30 to 40 percent of them fatal. In 2001, volunteer Ellen Roche died after inhaling hexamethonium, an experimental asthma treatment funded by the National Institutes of Health at Johns Hopkins University. In 2006, after passing animal testing, TGN 1412, a monoclonal antibody developed by the German company TeGenero as a potential rheumatoid arthritis treatment, went to human trials in England. Six young men recruited online by U.S.-based company Parexel were given TGN 1412 in doses hundreds of times lower than those given to animals. The men experienced severe reactions, with multiple organ breakdowns. One man's head swelled to three times its normal size, encouraging the media to label him "Elephant Man." A twenty-one-year-old young student suffered heart, liver and kidney failure, pneumonia, septicemia and gangrene and had all his toes and several fingers amputated. Immunologist Richard Powell of Nottingham University detected definite signs of lymphatic cancer and the *Times Online* (Leppard 2006) bluntly reported: "Elephant Man drug victims told to expect early death."

Although these and other drugs that caused adverse reactions in humans were all tested on other animals first, pro-vivisectionist groups use these cases to call for increased animal experimentation and minimize risks to human health. For example, the English group ProTest describes the 55,600 fatal hearts attributed to Vioxx as an "incredibly rare" side effect. Vivisection lobby groups focus solely on promoting animal research, even though it has been shown to be misleading, and ignore the search for alternatives.

Vivisectionists deride critics as uninformed animal lovers or violent terrorists. In reality, widespread opposition to vivisection exists within scientific and medical communities, exemplified by the Physicians Committee for Responsible Medicine. Similarly, Dr. David Horrobin (2003), Professor of Medicine at the Universite de Montreal, criticized animal models as poor representations of disease in humans, considered such tests a waste of resources and described current biomedical research as "an internally self-consistent universe with little contact with medical reality." Dr. Robert Sharp, formerly senior research chemist at London's Royal Postgraduate Medical School, resigned his position over animal testing and became scientific director of the International Association Against Painful Experiments on Animals (IAAPE). The IAAPE has consultative status with the United Nations, funds research into alternatives to vivisection and undercover investigations of cruelty in laboratories, and established World Day for Laboratory Animals (April 24) in 1979 (since expanded into World Lab Animal Week by the National Anti-Vivisection Society). The IAAPE's website documents "101 Misleading Results" derived from animal experimentation.

In a seminal review article, Major E. Matt Ritter, M.D., and Colonel Mark W. Bowyer, M.D., of the National Capital Area Medical Simulation Center and the Norman M. Rich Department of Surgery of the Uniformed Services University of the Health Sciences criticized use of live animals for trauma and casualty training. They consider animals "poor surrogates for human anatomy" and say their use "raises ethical issues, as well as not allowing for repetitive practice" (Ritter and Bower 2005). Nevertheless, Canada's military continues using animals in such procedures.

Vivisectionists claim their work is essential for medical progress. Animal advocates also want to save humans from terrible diseases such as cancer or AIDS. Yet much animal experimentation that counts as "medical research" is not concerned with these vital initiatives. Animal Alliance (n.d.) states: "according to statistics released by the [CCAC], nearly two-thirds of all animal research carried out in Canada has little or nothing to do with curing disease or advancing human medicine." Many experiments involve testing commercial products such as cosmetics and cleaning products, which are not vital to human survival, as well as military research, where animals are used to develop new weapons to kill people. For decades, psychologists have used animals in grotesque experiments on maternal deprivation and "learned helplessness," repeating experiments done by others, perhaps using different animals or changing conditions slightly and producing results anyone could predict. Typically, toxicity tests are not done to find antidotes to accidental poisoning but merely to determine lethal doses in various animals. Corporations conduct such tests to provide themselves with legal protection when their products poison and kill humans. Most experiments are repetitive; for example, many merely determine toxic effects of the same substance on different animals. Such experiments constitute a large portion of animal testing and should be discontinued immediately. So should all stress and addictions testing, popular in psychology departments. Even where animals are used in medical experiments, they are often used to produce "me too" copies of existing drugs so different companies can sell their version under a different name for profit. Furthermore, when vivisectionists champion animal testing as a necessity for prescription medications, we should note that much of this is redundant, repeating tests already done by other corporations, which do not reveal their results due to commercial reasons. Also, vivisection is promoted because animals themselves are commodities that can turn a profit. Large animals cost thousands of dollars and even smaller specially produced, genetically modified animals can be very expensive. Millions of animals are used as research tools, produced and sold by corporations for impressive profits.

Even where medical research is involved, it is often redundant. For example, UBC uses guinea pigs for smoking experiments, although dangers of smoking are well-known. UBC also uses non-human primates in neurological experiments, subjecting rhesus macaques to Parkinson's disease research. The monkeys are deliberately brain-damaged to model the disease and then given methamphetamine and electroconvulsive shocks. Many, even among the scientific community, object to using non-human primates in such experiments because of their similarity to humans, the same fact that makes them desirable test subjects for others who have no such ethical qualms. However, most animal advocates believe that similarity to humans should not be the main criterion for objections to vivisection.

Canadian vivisectors use animals to study human addictions. For example, Dr. William Corrigal, formerly of University of Toronto's physiology department and the Centre for Addiction and Medical Health and now operating a private consulting firm, used studies on mice for his work on nicotine dependence. His collaborator, Dr. Marina Picciotto from Yale University, was designated "Vivisector of the Month" by PETA in August 2008. Picciotto received approval from the university research ethics board for "learned helplessness" experiments, already exhaustively explored by others:

> [Picciotto] measure[d] despair in mice by forcing them to swim in pools of water with no resting platform or by hanging them from their tails. For each group of mice, despair was measured by how little they were still willing to struggle to save themselves.
>
> In another study, Picciotto bored holes into rats' skulls, injected chemicals directly into their brains, and then decapitated the animals and froze their heads. In a study on

learned helplessness, she exposed mice to 360 inescapable shocks. And in yet another experiment, Picciotto deprived monkeys of fluids and then gave them Kool-Aid mixed with liquid nicotine as their sole source of fluid. The amount of nicotine ingested by one monkey reached the equivalent of smoking 17 packs of cigarettes per day. Picciotto conducted this experiment in order to determine how long people should wait after ingesting nicotine before having brain imaging performed — despite the fact that researchers went on to take brain images of human smokers in another experiment, which could have provided information without caging and drugging monkeys. (Chandna 2009)

Both the University of Toronto and Yale University were involved with pharmaceutical companies such as Targacept, using animals to develop drugs that affect nicotine receptors. Yale's Spring 2007 newsletter on "Innovations in Women's Health" showcased Picciotto's interest in studying anti-depressive effects of Chantix (called Champix in Canada), a drug developed to assist smokers quit their habit. Yet many people who took Chantix experienced severe depression and suicidal thoughts, and the U.S. Food and Drug Administration warned of suicide, aggressive and erratic behaviour (including one case linked to death).

Even where animals are genetically similar to humans, as with chimpanzees, and the purpose is serious, as with HIV/AIDS research, vivisection has been a failure, reflected in the fact that 166 Members of Parliament in the U.K. signed a petition in 2006 to ban primate research not only because it caused tremendous suffering to animals but because it was bad science. Neurochemist Dr. Gill Langley, scientific advisor to the British government, European Commission and the Organisation for Economic Co-operation and Development, has examined problems of extrapolating to humans from data derived from primates, those animals who are closest to humans and thus, presumably, the best animal models. Langley (2006) notes "highly significant differences between the species in terms of genetics, molecular biology, pharmacology, physiology, absorption, distribution, metabolism and excretion and in reactions to drugs and chemicals" and concludes that although some predictions can be made they can only be confirmed by human trials. She also notes a 2004 U.S. Food and Drug Administration review that finds novel drugs tested on animals for years have only an 8 percent chance of proceeding to market: "The main causes of the 92% failure-rate are safety concerns and lack of effectiveness in humans, despite tests on primates and other animals. Indeed the FDA refers specifically to the limitations of animal toxicology and animal models for assessing drug efficacy."

While proponents say vivisection brought significant advances, many were actually discovered previously by other means and only later "validated" by animal tests (Greek and Greek 2000). Rejecting claims that vivisection is necessary for medical knowledge relevant to humans, Greek and Greek stress that animals are poor models for humans because they differ on cellular and molecular levels where disease occurs, do not naturally suffer from human diseases and because each species has a different response not only to illness but also to drugs used to treat illness. These factors render data derived from vivisection "misleading, unnecessary [and] dangerous" (17). In many cases, drugs found to be safe for animals cause death in humans. Conversely, because all drugs will have a negative effect on some animal, many useful drugs could be missed. They describe how many important medical advances were actually delayed due to animal experiments that took researchers down fruitless paths. They maintain that most medical knowledge has come from clinical observation and autopsies and argue that alternatives to vivisection exist in the form of in vitro research, work with stem cells, mathematical modelling, epidemiology, computer research, genetic research, diagnostic imaging and postmarketing drug surveillance.

Professor Christine Mummery, working in developmental biology at the University of Leiden, reported to the British Pharmacological Society that using embryonic human stem cells to create human heart cells provides a better alternative to animal tests, saving time and efforts, preventing dangerous or ineffective drugs from being developed and avoiding loss of drugs that might be effective in humans but that adversely affect animals. Mummery said stem cell research could completely transform drug development and described research in Europe as being "light years... away" from conditions in the U.S., where stem cell work is linked to debates about abortion and was underfunded by the Bush administration (Knight 2008).

Even when animal testing does suggest adverse reactions, companies conceal this information. The U.S. Food and Drug Administration, in the minutes to a 1995 meeting of the Recombinant DNA Advisory Committee of the National Institutes of Health, acknowledged that drug companies blocked dissemination of information on adverse reactions on the grounds that this was proprietary, despite risks to human subjects.

These facts indicate we should seriously reconsider using animals in research. Information on alternatives is available from organizations such as Interniche (International Network for Humane Education), the Physicians Committee for Responsible Medicine, the European Centre for the Validation of Alternative Methods, the New England Anti-Vivisection Society, the American Anti-Vivisection Society, the British Union for the Abolition of Vivisection, the British Anti-Vivisection Association and many others. Alternatives include autopsies, clinical studies, computer models, epidemiological studies, in vitro studies, tissue and cell culture work, artificial human skin for burn research and so on. The New England Anti-Vivisection Society promotes five hundred alternative humane education tools for use in classrooms, such as their Digital Frog for dissections, and report that students actually learn more and get better grades when they use these alternatives.

Animal experimentation reflects the political and economic context in which researchers compete for grants that enable them to publish papers and advance their careers. Billions of dollars support repetitive, pointless and cruel animal experiments, diverting attention from alternatives. Vivisection in Canada is a lucrative, extremely secretive and virtually unregulated industry (Montgomery 2000). While researchers who conduct animal experiments receive millions of dollars in public funding, it is impossible to obtain accurate accounting of how this money is spent. In-house committees that monitor animal use are controlled by those who do such research themselves. In this secretive and self-contained context, lobbyists for animal-exploitation industries find it useful to discursively construct animal rights advocates as fanatical and dangerous enemies. Characterizing anyone concerned with animals' well-being as an "animal rights extremist" and then exaggerating threats of violence allows researchers to evade public scrutiny of their activities and to operate with total secrecy and impunity.

10. MORAL SCHIZOPHRENIA AND CRUELTY

Another striking example of Canadians' moral schizophrenia lies in our utterly confused ideas about animal cruelty. The public becomes outraged over individual acts of sadism, while only minimal penalties exist, and institutionalized cruelties are perpetrated on a daily basis on a much greater scale. A few prominent cases indicate the nature of these individual cruelties.

Scenes of Cruelty

On December 30, 2007, Camrose resident Frank Snopek woke to sounds of a woman crying in his neighbour's yard. She explained she was looking after their home and had found it vandalized. Entering the house, Snopek saw "Nice cat, look in the microwave" written on the kitchen window and cabinets and the family cat inside the microwave. Snopek said the orange and black tabby, Princess, was "a nice little cat, very friendly," who "used to follow the kids down the street" (*Edmonton Journal* 2008). Four teenagers were charged with unlawfully killing an animal, unlawfully causing pain or suffering to an animal, break, enter and theft, mischief and possession of stolen property. Although Crown prosecutor John Laluk described the cat "screaming in the microwave for approximately 10 minutes while it is cooked to death," the perpetrators only received a hundred hours of community service, temporary restrictions on violent video games and a 9 p.m. curfew, and were sent to therapy (Gelinas 2008). Such lenient sentencing provoked gasps in the courtroom.

The impulses that motivated the Camrose teenagers also inspired John Ronald Hughes in Fernie, B.C. He claimed that while drunk on Valentine's Day, 2005, he sat on his girlfriend Sarah Kons' couch, which collapsed, injuring her cat. He woke Kons, who told him to break the cat's neck to end the pain and went back to sleep. Kons told the B.C. Provincial Court she was awakened by the sound of her microwave oven and found Hughes beside it, holding the cat, who was convulsing and screaming: "It was horrible... I started yelling at him, 'What are you doing?' and I was in complete shock. Like, something like that doesn't happen every day." Kons said Hughes hurled the cat at her. "I missed catching it and it hit the ground in front of me, gasping a few times while it was still convulsing, and died" (Rolfsen 2008). Kons became "suspicious" of Hughes' behaviour three weeks later when her second cat was injured. Kons returned home to find her cat's eyes glued shut, Hughes covered in scratches, patches of fur on the stove and blood in the bathroom. Initially, the Provincial Court acquitted Hughes of animal-cruelty charges, but Justice F.W. Cole of the B.C. Supreme Court overturned this, saying he did not believe Hughes acted to prevent the cat's suffering and noting Hughes' previous statements about hating cats and speculations about putting one in a microwave. Hughes' friends defended him, saying he "doesn't deserve all this attention" (CTV News June 30, 2006)

Another cat fell victim to Ontario College of Art and Design student Jesse Power, who in 2001 persuaded friends Anthony Wennekers and Matt Kaczorowski to join him in torturing and killing the animal and filming their actions. After they were charged with cruelty and mischief, Power's lawyer portrayed him as a vegan who designed the killing as an "artistic protest" against meat-eating. No animal rights group knew Power and a psychiatrist's report quoted Power's admission that he was trying to "spin" the torture as an art project. The report noted that Power was neither vegan nor vegetarian, that he was obsessed with handling dead animals and deliberately sought work at an abattoir. Bizarrely, Ontario Court Judge Ted Ormston said Power had not intended the cat to suffer and gave him a ninety-day weekends-only jail sentence. On appeal, Justice David Doherty upheld the sentence as what the law permitted but rejected Ormston's findings about Power's intent, saying Power engaged in "torture for torture's sake" (Blatchford 2003).

Like Hughes, Power had defenders. From 2001 to 2004, his friends harassed Freedom for Animals' Suzanne Lahaie, who kept attention on the case, leading to Kaczorowski's arrest in Vancouver. Power's friends followed her, videotaped her, made threatening telephone calls and vandalized her home. Police told Lahaie to expect harassment because of her activism. Power's friends Zev Asher and Linda Feesey made a film, *Casuistry: The Art of Killing a Cat*, which Asher (2001) said allowed the killers "a chance to tell their side of the story," as if debate existed. Asher, "wondering what all the fuss is about," attacked Lahaie as "a distressed creature… hysterical and seemingly unhinged," while detecting "an element of art" in Power's actions (Asher 2001; Savlov 2004).

In April 2008, University of Windsor business student Qu 'Luki' Li was charged with causing unnecessary suffering to an animal, after beating his Husky puppy Kiki so severely that the local humane society euthanized her. When police removed a coffee-table leg with the dog's hair embedded in it, Li explained he had been training her; witnesses testified they saw Li beating the dog. Many were outraged; an unrelated family, listed in the telephone book under a similar name, received threats and the University of Windsor's international student group feared attacks on foreign students.

In June 2007, a crying puppy, A.K., was found on a Windsor apartment balcony with infected wounds. His owner, Rony Salman, had severed the dog's ears to make him look menacing. While Salman's brutality is clear, his was a do-it-yourself approach to mutilations routinely done, albeit usually with anesthetic, by breeders who cut off dogs' ears and tails for cosmetic purposes. A.K.

was nursed back to health and rehomed. Salman, charged with animal cruelty under the Criminal Code, called himself an "animal lover" and complained he was "under a lot of pressure" from public outrage. While the maximum sentence was six months in jail, prohibition against owning pets for two years and a $2,000 fine, Salman's punishment was mild. While claiming to be "horrified" by Salman's brutality, Ontario Court Justice Guy Demarco gave him only a ninety-day sentence with a two-days-for-one credit for time in custody awaiting trial, so Salman was released. Afterwards, while Salman was imprisoned for burglary, one of his own ears was bitten off by another inmate. Scot Wortley, of the University of Toronto's Centre for Criminology, suggested Salman had received the same sort of prison justice given to sex offenders and pedophiles (Pearson 2008).

Private and Institutionalized Cruelty

These incidents and reactions to them, including outrage at the perpetrators' savagery, revenge against them, trivializations of violence towards animals and the courts' lenience are further indications of Canadians' moral schizophrenia about animal cruelty. While rightly condemning individual cruelties such as these, we must recognize historical, economic and social institutions that make other cruelties seem acceptable. Only a tiny fraction of the suffering animals endure at our hands comes from such deliberate acts of sadism. More comes from widely accepted, institutionalized operations of animal-exploitation industries: agriculture, fashion, entertainment, vivisection. The vast scale of these operations with all their mechanisms of intensive confinement, physical and psychological deprivations, invasive procedures of poisoning, burning, inducing diseases injuries and pain, inflicting abnormal conditions of aggression, anxiety and learned helplessness, and high-speed killing are cruelties we cannot fully comprehend. Although we rightly condemn killing individual animals, we accept similarly hideous practices inflicted on millions of animals in slaughterhouses. Procedures we condemn when done by individuals for sadistic pleasure we consider acceptable if conducted in laboratories as "research" or for "scientific" purposes, even if they produce no useful results and replicate experiments conducted elsewhere (Francione 2000). In such cases, abuse of animals for profit is normalized and considered completely acceptable. There is widespread agreement that any brutalities can be inflicted on those creatures we define as food animals or research tools, while those defined as pets should be treated differently. (It is not the species that counts: many cats and dogs are victimized in laboratories.) Complaining about individual acts of sadism while accepting or participating in far more extensive institutionalized cruelties against animals is simply a means of salving one's conscience.

We assume that individuals who delight in animals' suffering and death, turning their agonies into spectacles for amusement and gratification, are deranged psychopaths. However, events such as the Calgary Stampede or institutions such as Marineland in Niagara Falls, which imprisons gigantic ocean-dwelling mammals in concrete ponds, teach the public that animal abuse is fun. The idea that animals are nothing but resources for our use and acceptance of their institutionalized exploitation encourages acts of individual cruelty. One example of the public celebration of cruelty is the Thetford Chicken Massacre. This annual summer ritual is held near Thetford Mines, south of Quebec City, on property owned by local doctor Gaston Dorval, organized by his two sons and attended by crowds of drunken partygoers who chop off the heads of chickens and turkeys, throw the birds in the air and bet on where on a painted grid the birds' convulsing bodies will stop. Organizers created a Facebook page promoting their festive event, with photos and videos showing headless birds flopping on the ground and grinning participants guzzling beer and holding aloft the decapitated heads. Fun-loving partygoers posted messages expressing sentiments such as "Gotta kill them all!" and "finally, my first massacer [sic]." After the Quebec City humane society and PETA complained about this barbaric event in

2008, the Facebook page was removed and Dorval reluctantly said he would discontinue the festivities if he was threatened with criminal charges. However, he called it "hypocritical" of people to object to his parties because chickens suffer more in slaughterhouses. Dorval protested: "If this is torture, then we should close all slaughterhouses in Quebec.... They cut the chicken's throat and let them bleed to death. That's much more painful, but you don't see it.... People don't want to see how animals are killed" (Canwest News Service 2008). Dorval had a point, although obviously he lacks compassion for animals and regards closing slaughterhouses as an absurdity. Media reported the story as a joke, many guffawing that the practice "ruffled the feathers" of animal activists. Clearly, nothing could be as ridiculous as compassion for chickens and turkeys, animals who generally are regarded as mere meat-machines, life unworthy of life.

Antiquated Laws

Yet even in terms of this limited understanding of animal abuse, Canada's animal-cruelty laws are antiquated, remaining basically unchanged since the nineteenth century. Responding to public concern, in 1998, the Justice Department issued "Crimes Against Animals," a consultation paper on Canada's anti-cruelty laws, noting connections between violence towards animals and towards humans and suggesting revision. In 1999 Justice Minister Anne McLellan introduced Bill C-17 to remove animals from the property section of Canada's Criminal Code but an election was called and the bill died. Since then, the bill was reintroduced in various forms and designations in every Parliament over the last decade, but unified opposition from animal-exploitation industries, supported by Alliance and Conservative parties, blocked legislation each time as Parliament prorogued. In 2005, Senator John Bryden, supported by industry, introduced a private member's bill that increased penalties for cruelty convictions but welfare groups rejected it as seriously flawed, stressing that few convictions are ever achieved because of the Criminal

Code's many loopholes. This bill, too, died but Bryden reintroduced it as S-203. In 2006, MP Mark Holland introduced a private member's bill, C-373, as an alternative. Holland called Bryden's industry-supported bill "misguided" and "diversionary," saying it would preserve all the Criminal Code's loopholes that let abuse continue while seeming to address it through stiffer penalties for the few cases that bring convictions. Holland's bill died when the election was called but he reintroduced it again as C-229, calling it "unthinkable" that Canadian cruelty laws were fundamentally unchanged since 1892 and urging the government to "bring Canada's animal cruelty laws into the 21st Century" (Holland 2008). However, Bryden's industry-backed bill passed with support of the Conservatives, Liberals and Bloc Quebecois, despite a petition from 130,000 Canadians and opposition from all animal welfare groups. Steve Carroll, CEO of the Canadian Federation of Humane Societies said:

> Canadians should be offended and outraged that the government and the official opposition supported a bill that takes 1892 legislation and simply adjusts it for inflation by merely increasing the penalties…. This bill will do nothing to improve protection for animals from cruelty and abuse. (Marketwire 2008)

The IFAW (2008b) called Canada's anti-cruelty legislation "woefully inadequate," ranking at the bottom of comparisons with countries with animal protection laws. Several flaws exist in Canadian legislation. Canada does not even clearly define "animal" while other countries are explicit. Unlike others, our cruelty provisions only apply to animals "kept for a lawful purpose," so Canada offers almost no protection for wild and stray animals because they are not considered anyone's property. Welfare groups say this antiquated view of animals as mere property must be revised, that all animals deserve protection and that crimes against animals should be covered in a distinct section of the Criminal Code.

Although animal fighting is illegal in Canada, individuals must be present in order to be charged and, unlike other countries, breeding, training and profiting from fighting animals are not illegal here (so U.S. football player Michael Vick would not have been charged in Canada for his involvement in dog-fighting). These loopholes allow abuse to continue even when police have evidence. For example, in 2005, the RCMP and SPCA seized twenty-five dogs and clear evidence of an organized fighting operation but had to return the dogs because no one would cooperate with the investigation. The *Vancouver Sun* (2007) reported that there had been not a single conviction for organized dog-fighting in the province and quoted RCMP Constable Annie Linteau: "It's a horrible 'sport' of the gladiator-type era…. You are pitting two animals together for the sole purpose of watching one of them die. It's one of the sickest forms of betting or gaming that I can imagine."

Canada's Criminal Code makes it is almost impossible to prosecute neglect because the Code refers to "willful neglect," meaning it must be predetermined, whereas in other countries prosecutors do not face the difficult tasks of proving willful intent and motives. As a result, over 99 percent of acts of cruelty go unpunished in Canada.

Consequences for convictions remain light. Incarceration lengths and maximum fines are among the lowest, and offenders are not required to pay restitution for welfare groups that care for abused animals. While many countries impose permanent prohibitions against owning animals for convicted abusers, Canada only prevents offenders from owning animals for two years (maximum), the shortest time of all countries surveyed by IFAW.

Proposed changes to the law were modest, including increased penalties for conviction and some recognition that animals are sentient beings and not simply inanimate objects (designed to forestall abusers from claiming they are allowed to damage their own property). Changes were designed to help facilitate prosecution of actions causing "unnecessary" pain and suffering. This was understood as that inflicted on animals by individuals to deliberately cause pain;

changes in legislation would not affect suffering routinely inflicted upon animals in agricultural and research industries. Inflicting pain and suffering upon animals would remain acceptable if it served lawful purposes. Reform of anti-cruelty laws posed no threat to animal exploitation industries.

Industry Opposition

Animal-exploitation industries worried that any increased protection of animals would make them vulnerable. Recognizing that any reconsideration of cruelty and the status of animals posed a potential threat in the sense that it might lead to more serious regulation in the future, industries depicted themselves as under attack from animal rights "extremists" and demanded blanket exemptions, despite the fact that such exemptions already exist. Knowing that inclusion of "lawful excuse" in proposed legislation would still permit animal abuse in activities such as farming, fishing, hunting, trapping and vivisection, animal-exploitation industries nevertheless fought any modification to existing laws. Groups opposing updated laws included the fur industry, hunting groups, meat, dairy and egg industries, animal breeders and vivisectors. In short, all groups that profit from animal-exploitation blocked efforts to stop cruelty. These industries, based on suffering, recognized that any change in public attitudes towards animals, any recognition of animals' ethical standing or of increased human responsibilities towards animals represents a potential threat to their own interests.

Opponents used wild exaggerations and deliberate lies. Groups such as the Canadian Cattlemen's Association, Chicken Farmers of Canada, the Alberta Farm Care Association, the Horse Council of British Columbia and the Agricultural Institute of Canada lobbied against new laws, misrepresenting changes, claiming they would stop all legal uses of animals and that anyone working with animals would be prosecuted. The Ontario Federation of Anglers and Hunters not only argued for keeping animal cruelty under the Criminal

Code's property provisions and opposed any changes concerning killing and harming animals but also denounced restrictions on animal fighting. Sally Galsworthy, a University of Western Ontario microbiologist, called the bill "dangerous" (Tesher 2001). Through the 1990s, Alliance and Conservative Party MPs said new protection represented "humanization" of animals and would undermine human rights. The Association of Universities and Colleges of Canada demanded that animals should remain as property under the Criminal Code and be denied any protection in their own right so university researchers could continue to experiment on them. The Canadian Institutes of Health Research and the Natural Sciences and Engineering Research Council argued, incorrectly, that activists could use improved legislation to prosecute scientists using animals in research, driving biotechnology and pharmaceutical industries out of Canada.

Alliance MPs and industry lobbyists warned of a "hidden agenda" by animal rights activists, despite the fact that proposed changes did not concern animals' rights and would leave basic structures of exploitation unchanged. Fur industry lobbyist Alan Herscovici said updating anti-cruelty legislation was an attack on human rights, a dangerous trick by animal activists comparable to terrorists who attacked New York and Washington on September 11, 2001. Although such outlandish distortions and propaganda so obviously served Herscovici's own financial interests, industry lobbyists again defeated any changes. Those who profit from institutionalized abuse and killing of animals deliberately exaggerated the effect of proposed amendments and vilified everyone concerned about animal welfare as radicals, extremists and terrorists. Such intense opposition to modest reform of animal cruelty legislation suggests that even while those in animal exploitation industries defend them as normal and acceptable, they recognize their vicious and exploitative character and understand that they must be constantly on guard against any potential changes, no matter how slight.

Despite virtually unlimited exploitation of animals in Canada and the extreme backwardness of our laws concerning their treatment, Canada portrays itself as a civilized and decent nation. In January 2009, a Canadian government delegation lobbied European Union officials against restricting imports of Canadian goods produced from animals. Their visit was preceded by an official document emailed to Members of the European Parliament concerning Canadian government policies on commercial exploitation of wildlife. That document said: "Canada is committed to, and has a long history of setting humane standards for animal welfare" and has "strong legislation to protect the welfare of animals," including severe penalties under the Criminal Code.

In February 2009, six of Canada's major animal welfare organizations wrote an open letter to Prime Minister Stephen Harper, protesting government misrepresentations of treatment of animals in Canada (Poultry Site News 2009). They rejected claims made in January, arguing that Canada lags far behind many countries in animal-protection legislation. They noted that Canada does not have an animal welfare act and that recent amendments leave Canada's Criminal Code virtually unchanged from 1892, that it does not define "animal," offers little protection for wild or stray animals, allows training animals to fight each other and contains loopholes and outdated language that result in conviction rates of under 1 percent for those charged with cruelty. Stephanie Brown, director for the Canadian Coalition for Farm Animals, observed that Canada's new $1.3 billion five-year agricultural policy, Growing Forward Framework Agreement, fails to even mention the words "animal welfare," indicating the level of government concern for this issue. Noting that most Canadians support animal welfare and that our laws should reflect that, Rob Laidlaw, director of Zoocheck Canada said: "Canada is still in the dark ages when it comes to animal welfare." Rebecca Aldworth, director of Humane Society International/Canada stated:

Canada is one of the worst places in the industrialized

world for animals.... Our outdated animal protection laws facilitate serious abuses of animals. From the beating and shooting of seal pups to the proliferation of puppy mills, to the mass force-feeding of geese and ducks to the widespread use of leghold traps — millions of animals are routinely subjected to extreme cruelty in Canada.

11. ENTANGLED OPPRESSIONS

As noted in Chapter One, many dismiss animal rights by saying we should be concerned about humans first. In fact, these concerns are inseparable. While humans profit from animal exploitation, in all cases examined in this book, oppression of animals also has negative consequences for humans, ranging from attacks or transmission of disease from exotic pets, misleading information from vivisection, ecological damage from the fur trade, economic losses from government determination to prop up the seal hunt or simply the brutalization and degradation of character associated with rodeos and hunting. Calling for a deeper appreciation of all forms of life and greater sympathy with animals, Henry Salt (1894: 88) pointed out:

> To advocate the rights of animals is far more than to plead for compassion or justice towards the victims of ill-usage; it is not only, and not primarily, for the sake of the victims that we plead, but for the sake of mankind itself… it is ourselves, our own vital instincts, that we wrong, when we trample the rights of the fellow-beings, human or animal, over whom we chance to hold jurisdiction.

The connection between mistreatment of animals and dangers for humans is nowhere more apparent than in the area that also constitutes the most widespread form of animal abuse: using animals for food. These practices create serious problems for health and the environment. Looking at global meat production reveals important links between animal rights and other social justice issues.

Antibiotics

Factory farming involves extensive use of drugs to treat animals: confining a million animals in close proximity in unsanitary conditions with poor ventilation creates ideal means for spreading diseases. To control disease, animals receive high doses of antibiotics. The rationale for giving antibiotics to animals is to prevent disease but this might no longer be working: lower rates of bacteria are found in animals fed antibiotic-free brands (Price, Johnson, Vailes and Silbergold 2005). However, perhaps 90 percent of antibiotics are given to promote rapid growth (Khachatourians 1998). Chemical-laced factory farm waste pollutes nearby water sources, including human drinking water. Chemical residue remains in animals' flesh after they are slaughtered, passing drug-resistant microbes on to those who consume animals' flesh and milk, transferring this resistance to bacteria in human bodies. In Britain in 2005, a new antibiotic-resistant strain of bacteria, extended-spectrum beta-lactamase (ESBL)-producing E.coli, unknown before 2000, infected thousands of humans, causing blood poisoning and urinary tract infections in elderly or chronically ill patients, killing many. Even if antimicrobial resistance develops in bacteria harmless to humans, it is still problematic because resistant genes can pass to other, deadly pathogens.

Drug-resistant bacteria entail serious implications for treatment of human diseases and adds tens of billions of dollars to health care costs. In 1999, the U.S. National Academy of Science's Institute of Medicine estimated that treating antibiotic-resistant infections in that country cost $30 billion a year (National Institute of Allergy and Infectious Diseases 1999). By encouraging antibiotic resistance, we set ourselves up for disaster by making ourselves more vulnerable to diseases (some of which will be generated and spread by the same system of animal agriculture that creates new pathogens).

The World Health Organization suggested strict regulation of antibiotic use in livestock and an immediate halt to using essential drugs for growth promotion. Banning non-therapeutic antibiotic use in livestock shows striking results. Denmark's 1999 ban significantly reduced antimicrobial resistance levels. In 2006 the European Union banned non-therapeutic antibiotic use in animals. Canada, placing agribusiness profits over public health, lags behind and only began studying the issue under the Canadian Integrated Program for Antimicrobial Resistance Surveillance in 2002.

Canada approves growth hormones to enlarge animals for sale. These are carcinogenic in humans, and the government approved their use over strong protests from its own top scientists, as in the case of Revalor H, a hormone implanted subcutaneously to increase growth. The government approved it over objections from Margaret Haydon and Shiv Chopra, senior scientists at Health Canada. Evidence shows that the drug induces premature puberty and ab-normal growth of mammary tissue in female calves, hugely enlarged prostate glands in male calves and abnormal growth of the thymus gland, which regulates the immune system. Despite a gag-order from Health Canada, Haydon warned a Senate agriculture committee that her supervisors ignored human health concerns raised by all scientists in her group. Shortly before, six Health Canada scientists complained of being pressured to approve drugs they considered dangerous, including Monsanto's BST, a genetically engineered drug to increase milk production in cows.

Pollution

One problem of factory farms is concentrated "waste" (excrement). Waste is beneficial as fertilizer but factory farms produce huge amounts, which cannot be absorbed into the soil or managed at such high levels. Since each animal produces much more waste than a per-son does, a factory containing a million animals can generate the waste equivalent of a town, or even a small country. Canada's pigs produce enough waste every twenty-two days to fill Toronto's Skydome (CTV News 2002), and North America's industrial farms produce over a billion tons of waste annually. Liquid hog waste is sprayed into vast, open lagoons or spread onto fields. However, this seeps into streams and wells and poisons wildlife habitats and human drinking water. It also produces clouds of ammonia; circulated as rain, this contributes to growth of algae in nearby streams, rivers and lakes and chokes off life in those water systems. Manure lagoons cause environmental disasters, as disease-causing bacteria spill into rivers and groundwater used for drinking. A North Carolina hog manure lagoon burst in 1995, spilling 25 million gallons of contaminants, which killed 10 million fish and affected hundreds of thousands of acres of coastal areas. In northern New York in 2005, 11 million litres of cow manure burst through a retaining wall and flowed into the Black River and Black River Bay, which flows into Lake Ontario, killing hundreds of thousands of fish. People living near factory farms are affected by clouds of toxic gas and dust, as well as overpowering odours, that result in respiratory and gastrointestinal problems. Metz Farms in St. Marie, New Brunswick, raises 10,000 pigs at a time, and keeps millions of gallons of untreated waste in a hole in the ground, causing risks for local people, who developed weeping sores that would not heal due to chemical exposure from the pig farm kilometres away. The Canadian Medical Association asked governments for a moratorium on hog farms, at least until health risks were studied, but corporate farms block research.

Livestock production is a major factor in water pollution through waste, fertilizers, pesticides, chemicals, antibiotics and hormones. It reduces biodiversity through deforestation, land degradation, pollution, climate change, overfishing, degradation of coastal regions and introduction of alien species. The Pew Commission (2006) examined U.S. animal feeding operations in areas of public health, environment, animal welfare and rural communities, noting significant problems: increased antibiotic-resistant bacteria due to overuse of antibiotics, reduced air quality, contamination of rivers, streams and coastal waters with concentrated animal waste, animal welfare issues and negative impacts on social structure and economy of farming regions.

Intensive livestock production creates significant air and water pollution, causing disease and respiratory problems, including asthma, not only among workers but among those living far from livestock operations. In addition to pollution of waterways from animal manure, runoff carries antibiotics, hormones, pesticides, veterinary pharmaceuticals and heavy metals, especially zinc and copper, which are added as micronutrients to animal feed. The Pew Commission expressed concern at disproportionately large usage of fossil fuel, industrial fertilizer and chemicals as well as high levels of greenhouse gases, toxic gases, bioaerosols containing microorganisms and human pathogens and foul odours produced by livestock operations. Focus on monocrop production to feed animals has created soil erosion and water depletion, requiring heavy fertilizer use and contributing to global warming. Extensive use of pesticides and herbicides has led to loss of biodiversity, with further ecological implications, as well as to the poisoning of humans, seen in epidemics of cancer and birth defects.

Wasting Resources

Huge amounts of land, water and grain are required to maintain livestock; consequences include massive air, water and soil pollution and degradation. A finite amount of agricultural land exists; much of it goes to livestock production, now over 21 billion animals annually. Over a quarter of the world's land area supports livestock production, with a third of total arable land devoted to foodcrop production for livestock; livestock production occupies 70 percent of all agricultural land and 30 percent of the world's land surface. Extensive pasture and rangeland areas are degraded by overgrazing, compaction and livestock-related erosion. Although industries claim that animals are raised on marginal land unsuitable for humans, in fact, animals are increasingly raised on lands that could support humans and fed with cereals and grains that humans could eat. For example, 90 percent of the world's soybeans are grown for animal food and 40 percent of the world's grain (and over 70 percent of the grain in the U.S.) is fed to animals.

Feeding grain to animals who are slaughtered for their flesh is not only a cruel, wasteful and inefficient system as humans suffer famine and malnutrition but directly contributes to human poverty by marginalizing small farmers and driving them from their land. Vegan diets can support much larger numbers of people using far fewer resources. The Vegan Society (n.d.) claims that a typical omnivorous European diet requires five times the land required for a varied vegan diet. British organization Vegfam estimates that a vegan Britain could be self-sufficient on just 25 percent of its presently available agricultural land, stating that a ten-acre farm could feed sixty people with soybeans, twenty-four with wheat, ten with corn but only two with cows' flesh. Livestock production has a huge impact on the planet (Steinfeld, Gerber, Wassenaar, Castel, Rosales and de Haan 2006). By 2025, 64 percent of the human population will face water shortages, yet we continue to devote over 8 percent of global human water use to livestock, mainly for irrigating crops to feed animals.

Meat production depletes other vital resources. Over a third of all fossil fuel and all raw materials used in the U.S. are devoted to animal industries. These industries also require massive amounts of water. Whereas 1,000 litres of water are needed to produce one kilo of wheat, it takes between 2000 and 4000 litres to produce a kilo of milk, 5,000 for a kilo of cheese and 11,000 litres to produce just one "quarter-pounder" hamburger. Massive, industrial-scale livestock operations are a massive drain on the world's diminishing water supplies. Globally, millions of small farmers who grow fodder for animals to produce milk are using unsustainable amounts of water from underground reservoirs that are running dry and cannot be replenished. Animal agriculture is fast-tracking hundreds of millions of people not only towards drought, displacement and greater poverty in urban slums but also towards mass starvation.

Global Warming

Along with consumerism and militarism, electricity generation and transport, meat production is a major cause of global warming. Livestock production accounts for 18 percent of greenhouse gas emissions, more than transportation, and generates much higher levels of particular gases involved in global warming and acid rain. The United Nations Food and Agricultural Organization (2006) found world livestock production responsible for 9 percent of the world's carbon dioxide, 37 percent of methane, 64 percent of ammonia and 65 percent of nitrous-oxide emissions, nearly a fifth of world greenhouse gas emissions, more than the global transportation sector combined. Additionally, rainforests are being cut to provide grazing for cows and to grow crops to feed them. In South America, livestock production drives deforestation, with 70 percent of previously forested land turned into pasture for livestock, and much of the rest is used for crops to feed animals. Increasingly, marginal areas are being used, leading to desertification. This not only devastates the forests' biodiversity and eliminates their role in absorbing carbon dioxide and producing oxygen but adds additional greenhouse gases. Consequences of global warming include flooding, extreme weather, population displacements, war and mass extinctions. In 2004 World Watch linked consumption of animals to all major forms of environmental damage, including air pollution, biodiversity loss, climate change, deforestation, erosion and water pollution, as well as to their social effects, including the destruction of communities, social injustice and spread of disease. In 2007, the Military Advisory Board, a panel of eleven retired U.S. admirals and generals issued their report, "National Security and the Threat of Climate Change," for the Center for Naval Analyses. The report described climate change as a serious national security threat with the potential for human and natural disasters on an unprecedented scale, likely to exacerbate already-marginal living conditions for much of the world's population and act as a threat multiplier, increasing political instability, increased authoritarianism and extremism as food and water become scarce, diseases spread and populations move in search of basic resources. The U.N. advised that the livestock sector should be a focus for environmental policy and warned that an expected doubling of the current livestock population (60 billion) would negate any improvements from efficiencies in other sectors or conservation measures and render it impossible to achieve emission reductions necessary to avoid global disaster.

Comparing fossil fuel use in producing and processing various foods, including operation of agricultural machinery, producing food for livestock and methane and nitrous oxide emissions from livestock, University of Chicago geophysicists Gideon Eshel and Pamela Martin (2006) demonstrated that the meat-based average American diet produces one and a half tons more greenhouse gases compared to a vegan diet and concluded that a vegan or even vegetarian diet is a more significant step in reducing global warming than driving a hybrid car. Such findings prompted economist Dr Rajendra Pachauri, recognized world authority on climate change, joint winner of the 2007 Nobel Peace Prize and chair of the United Nations Intergovernmental Panel on Climate Change, to urge people to stop eating meat as a method of taking personal action to reduce global warming: "In terms of immediacy of action and the feasibility of bringing about reductions in a short period of time, it clearly is the most attractive opportunity" (Jowett 2008). The same year, renowned climatologist Dr. James Hansen of the U.S. National Aeronautics and Space Administration warned that we have only four years to act on climate change and advised adopting a vegetarian diet. In January 2009, Britain's National Health Service began promoting meat-free menus in hospitals to cut greenhouse gas emissions.

Human Health

In addition to negative environmental effects, meat-based diets threaten human health, increasing rates of chronic diseases, including heart disease, stroke and some cancers, in contrast to diets higher in vegetables, fruits and grains (Walker et al. 2005). Canadians whose diets are is high in animal products (meat, cheese, butter, eggs, milk, ice cream) consume more saturated fats and have higher cholesterol levels, associated with heart attacks, higher blood pressure, obesity, coronary artery disease, hypertension, diabetes, mellitus and various cancers. T. Colin Campbell, former senior science advisor to the American Institute for Cancer Research states: "The vast majority of all cancers, cardiovascular diseases, and other forms of degenerative illness can be prevented simply by adopting a plant-based diet" (Robbins 2001: 39). A study by the American Institute for Cancer Research and World Cancer Research Fund (1997), with participation from the World Health Organization, the U.N.'s Food and Agricultural Organization, International Agency on Research in Cancer and the U.S. National Cancer Institute, in which 120 researchers analyzed data from 4,500 research studies concluded that 70 percent of cancer can be prevented largely by adopting a vegetarian diet. In Western societies the average person consumes twice the recommended daily intake of protein. Emphasis on consuming animal products has created epidemic-levels of heart disease, cancer, diabetes and obesity. Growing costs of treating these conditions have caused a crisis in Canada's public health system. Yet, these conditions could be prevented or alleviated by healthy nutritious vegan diets, freeing resources for other essential services.

Intensive production, now the dominant model, confines billions of animals in concentrated feeding operations and factory farms; overcrowding of animals creates psychological and physical stress, aggression and disease while profit-maximization has led to such "efficiencies" as turning herbivorous animals into carnivores by feeding them remains of members of their own species, causing human health-disasters such as mad cow disease, which killed at least 150 people, mainly in Britain. Diseases such as avian flu and swine flu also show the ability to jump species; it is only a matter of time before a global animal-based pandemic kills massive numbers of humans.

Meat Consumption and Human Problems

Meat consumption increased substantially in the twentieth century, promoted by industries that proclaim the necessity of eating flesh. Our meat-intensive diet is unprecedented in history but is now considered the norm and imagined to be the right of all. As the growing human population is encouraged to see consumption of vast quantities of animals' flesh as a marker of status, health and modernity, livestock populations have been increased sharply. Livestock production tripled since the mid-twentieth century, and consumption is soaring, driven by the fast-food industry. Production will double again from 1990 levels by 2050. These trends continue despite extensive evidence that a meat-based diet is environmentally disastrous and unhealthy for humans. Raising livestock as commodities has exacerbated the global environmental crisis, social injustice and hunger. Acquiring meat not only entails killing animals but requires violence against humans to maintain the vastly inefficient and destructive global meat system, causing displacement by capital-intensive agribusiness of small farmers who cannot afford the necessary chemicals and oil-using equipment, murder of Indigenous peoples and peasants in the rainforests and exploitation of workers in slaughterhouses. Globally, millions of poor farmers are pushed off their land into urban slums as huge areas come under ownership by local elites and giant corporations, supported by the World Bank and the IMF, dedicated to producing meat for export or food for livestock. Modern capitalist agribusiness exacerbates hunger rather than solving it.

In our world millions of people suffer malnutrition and starvation; approximately 25,000 humans die each day from hunger and malnutrition-related causes, In 2009, the U.N. Food and Agriculture Organization stated that over one billion people are chronically hungry. Enough food is produced to feed the present human population, but availability is manipulated by greed and profit-seeking, and resources are wasted on producing meat for wealthy consumers. However, current production methods are inefficient and unsustainable; a growing fast-food industry and desire to emulate the Standard American Diet, with its emphasis on animal products, will further strain this system and continue to deprive the world's poor of food. Increasing our already colossal consumption of meat means even more death, deforestation, displacement, disease and deprivation. Meat is abundant and seemingly cheap but is costing the earth.

Vegetarianism and Veganism

Those who have ethical concerns for animals and care about the human and ecological impact of meat production will not only commit themselves to support for long-term cultural and political processes of change but will also seek to modify their own behaviour. In doing so, we must address the most extensive form of animal abuse, using them for food. This inevitably leads to a consideration of vegetarianism. Vegetarianism suggests a plant-based diet but the term has been diluted to include "vegetarians" who consume a variety of animal products, including flesh. In order to introduce more consistency, the term veganism was proposed by Donald Watson in 1944 to indicate those who attempt to minimize exploitation and cruelty and to live without consuming animals for food, clothing or other purposes. A pacifist and conscientious objector, Watson considered veganism the expression of a more compassionate approach to life. Adopting a vegan diet, one free not only of flesh but of milk, eggs, cheese and all other animal products, is a sensible approach to not only reducing animal suffering but to countering negative environmental impacts. Many resources exist to make this easy: vegan cookbooks and products are widely available, vegetarian societies exist in most major cities and the Internet provides a wide range of information.

Many dismiss veganism and animal rights as sentimental concerns of affluent people who think individual consumer choices are sufficient to achieve an equitable society. Of course, these objections are made by people who themselves wish to continue to exploit animals by eating or wearing them, and, like all who seek to retain power and privilege, they try to marginalize their critics. They emphasize that eating meat is "natural" despite the fact that, physiologically, humans are not well-suited to consuming flesh and that the bulk of human diet throughout the course of our evolution has been plants. Some worry that vegan diets are unhealthy but balanced vegan diets are nutritionally adequate. They do not require expensive, processed meat substitutes as sources of protein but include traditional foods of most peasant societies, such as beans, rice and tofu. A plant-based diet is nutritionally adequate, healthy, more environmentally sound and less expensive than the average North American diet with its heavy concentration on animal-derived foods.

As for the typical objection against animal rights and veganism that human problems must be solved first before any concern can be expressed for the plight of animals, it is unclear how eating animals is an expression of concern for humans. Also, such prioritizing of suffering would be considered unacceptable if the victims were all humans. Furthermore, it is a mistake to assume that those who are concerned about animals are unconcerned with humans; there is no reason why these concerns cannot be expressed simultaneously. One can easily work on other issues while being vegan. Those who claim that they eat animals because they care about humans conveniently overlook the massive impact on humans of the global animal-agriculture industry, in terms of environmental degradation, human health problems, impoverishment and starvation.

Some who are critical of the status quo propose alternatives to veganism that claim to go "beyond factory farming" or to offer "humane meat" or other "sustainable" animal products. Such alternatives may offer support to small farmers rather than corporate agriculture but offer little or nothing from an animal rights perspective. For example, in 2009, a major initiative on the Beyond Factory Farming Coalition website was the campaign to save Atlantic Canada's only remaining slaughterhouse as a means to preserve the region's beef industry. Purveyors of "humane meat" suggest that it is acceptable to kill animals for food if they have lived a happy life. Yet these animals are still considered property and their lives are prematurely ended, usually in the same slaughterhouses that kill others who not raised "humanely." Designations such as "free range," "free run" or "cage free" are vaguely defined, and, in many cases, animals raised in these conditions suffer almost as much as those who are raised according to standard practices. While any diminution of suffering, no matter how slight, can be said to be an improvement for the victims, an animal rights perspective does not simply seek modifications in the abusive treatment of animals but, rather, objects to their use. Recognition of the inherent value of all sentient beings leads not simply to the call for "humane treatment" but to the abolition of animal exploitation.

Simply in terms of the amount of land available and the price, "humane meat" is not a feasible option for more than a small niche market. The real benefit of "humane meat" is to producers, who are able to charge premium prices to affluent consumers who wish to consume animal products but salve their consciences. Elite consumers purchase a sense of moral superiority by paying premium prices to make suffering seem less apparent while marketing campaigns present the victims as happy ones. Animal-exploitation industries have always employed a discourse of love and caring for animals as a strategy to conceal their exploitation. "Humane slaughter" is just the latest version, an oxymoron that is the denial of animals' suffering and death. Eating animals is the contradiction of all progressive values, while veganism is an expression of commitment to them.

Veganism is not simply a diet but is the attempt to minimize the suffering and death of animals generally, so vegans oppose all the forms of exploitation described in the chapters of this book. Thus, vegans not only oppose using animals for food but also oppose the mistreatment of animals in entertainment spectacles such as rodeos, the killing of animals in trophy hunting and the use of animals in vivisection. Just as they avoid the use of animal products in their diet, vegans avoid clothing made from animals' skins or hair. However, veganism is not simply a "lifestyle option" or "green consumerism" focused on purchasing expensive eco-friendly products. Veganism puts into practice the basic ideas of animal rights, that animals should not be regarded simply as resources for human use and that they are beings with inherent value whose moral status is comparable to that of humans.

Veganism is not just a personal choice but a political one. It is the logical outcome of the recognition that animals are not property but individual beings who have their own interests, which should be considered. It is an ethical commitment, a symbolic gesture and a statement of principle, the rejection of hierarchy, domination and op-pression, an acknowledgement of the inherent value of other beings. Veganism is expression of animal rights philosophy through the effort to reduce, as much as possible, the exploitation of animals. Becoming vegan expresses a commitment to minimize harm and avoid a diet based on misery and demonstrates compassion and concern for the well-being of others. Individual actions are insufficient to change entrenched systems of domination, and consumerist actions alone cannot challenge the fundamental basis of the system but these are not arguments against veganism. We recognize that individual com-mitments will not dismantle racism or patriarchy, but this does not mean that progressive individuals should persist in racist or sexist practices. Individuals should make an effort to live in ways that are consistent with their values. Becoming vegan also plays a role in edu-cating others and drawing attention to the oppressive hierarchies that structure our world, not just speciesist ideology but corporate power and the capitalist institution that support it. As noted in Chapter One, historically, animal advocates have shown themselves to be supporters of other progressive movements, even as these other movements have failed to recognize the ethical case for animal rights.

Understanding that veganism is the basic response to a world structured by animal exploitation should not be misinterpreted as an assertion that it is a sufficient response. It is merely the first step in attempting to live in a way that is consistent with progressive values. An important part of veganism is the ethic of reducing harm and expressing concern for the well-being of others. Why maintain a diet based on misery?

More than a century ago, Salt (1894: 102–03) called for educational and legislative changes that would encourage an "enlightened sense of equality" to replace humanity's "selfish, aggressive tendencies." Significant advances will require a long period of cultural struggle and can only occur through fundamental policy changes. However, individual actions can have important effects. Rather than dismissing veganism as a privilege of the affluent, we must shift perception and recognize it as the only reasonable, humane, ethical and ecological option. Even those who refuse to recognize the plight of animals as a serious political issue and who endorse the most horrific suffering and exploitation of other beings as long as it ostensibly benefits humans must recognize that the global meat system is no benefit at all but a suicidal addiction that has brought us to the brink of disaster. Anyone concerned about human suffering should oppose a global meat industry that undermines millions of people's livelihoods, severely degrades the environment and consumes vast amounts of vital resources.

While Canada considers itself a compassionate society, a brief glance at how we obtain our food, our practices of pet-keeping, our outdated cruelty laws, the fur industry and seal hunt, our unregulated vivisection industry and practices such as trophy-hunting and rodeos, shows us a good deal about ourselves and what we find exciting, entertaining or amusing. All these pleasures are obtained at the expense of animals. We not only exploit them for food, usually without a second thought, but find stimulation, even humour, in their humiliation, pain and death. These facts raise disturbing questions about our society and about our own values, ethics and moral progress. While it is sufficiently important to consider how these practices reflect and perpetuate our alienation from other animals, we may note that self-interest and alienation from other forms of life extend into relationships with other humans. As Salt (1894: 103–04) observed, the case for animal rights is not simply a plea for mercy toward those other beings, but through realizing our fellowship with all nature, we will most truly become ourselves. This means not only opposing the practices of exploitation mentioned in the preceding chapters but overcoming the deeply rooted prejudices of humanism, our overwhelming sense of self-importance and our species solipsism, the belief that we are the only conscious and significant beings on the planet and that the rest of nature exists only as a collection of resources for our use. Darwin's recognition of continuity between ourselves and other animals has now been supplemented by extensive work in biology and ethology that indicates the complexity of animal consciousness and the depth of animals' emotional and social lives, their sense of self, memory, possession of culture, ability to use tools and capacity to use language. At the same time, ecofeminists have demonstrated that patriarchal ideologies and institutions are based on the entangled oppression of animals and women, and a few recognize that socialism must also involve animal liberation (Nibert 2002; Sanbonmatsu 2004). These findings represent nothing less than a fundamental transformation of our epistemological, moral and political universe. Furthermore, attitudes and practices of treating animals as means to our ends encourage us to see other humans the same way. This is manifested in exploitation of workers, relentless consumerism, desperation to acquire more goods at the expense of the environment, desire for profit at the expense of all other values and racism and hatred of otherness, rather than an ethical system based on compassion and equal consideration of interests. Those with enough courage to look into the mirror can see what exists now, not what must be, and if we do not like what we see there, we have the power and responsibility to change it.

REFERENCES

All online citations were current in September 2009, except where noted

Adams, Carol J. 2000. *The Sexual Politics of Meat*. New York: Continuum.

Aldworth, Rebecca. 2008. "Cover-Up Continues: DFO Restricting Journalists and Seal Hunt Observers Access to Today's Seal Hunt." Humane Society of the United States. <http://www.hsus.org/press_and_publications/press_releases/cover-up_continues_seal_hunt_ob-servation_permits_restricted_march_30_2008.html>

American Institute for Cancer Research/World Cancer Research Fund. 1997. *Food, Nutrition, and the Prevention of Cancer: A Global Perspective*. Washington, DC: American Institute for Cancer Research.

Animal Alliance. n.d. "Research." <http://www.cruelscience.ca/research.htm>

Animals Angels. 2007. "Investigation of Richelieu Meat Inc. April–June, 2007." External Report. <http://www.defendhorsescanada.org/pdf/richelieu2007.pdf>

Asher, Zev. 2001. "Specious Judgment and Other Oblique Definitions of the Word 'Casuistry.'" Cinemascope, May. <http://www.cinema-scope.com/cs21/spo_asher_festival.htm>

Bain, Jennifer. 2007. "The Real Deal About Veal." *Toronto Star*. April 4. <http://www.thestar.com/printArticle/199070>

Baumel, Syd. 2006. "Indecent Eggsposure: How Eggs are Laid in Canada." United Poultry Concerns. June 1. <http://www.upc-online.org/canada/60506eggs.html>

Beyond Factory Farming Coalition. n.d. "Vision and Mandate." <http://beyondfactoryfarming.org/who-we-are/vision-and-mandate>

Bisgould, Leslie, Wendy King and Jennifer Stoppard. 2001. *Anything Goes*.

Toronto: Animal Alliance of Canada.

Blatchford, Christie. 2003. "Cat Torture Was Not Art: Judges." *National Post*. June 14. <http://canada.com/national/story.asp?id=A831B73E-CB9B-4AAC-8DC5-81B1750AF0DD>

Bourdain, Anthony. 2001. *Kitchen Confidential*. New York: Harper.

Bourdieu, Pierre. 1984. *Distinction*. Cambridge: Harvard University Press.

Campbell, T. Colin, and Thomas M. Campbell II. 2006. *The China Study*. Dallas: BenBella Books.

Canadian Agri-Food Research Council. 1998. "Recommended Code of Practice for the Care and Handling of Farm Animals." <http://www.fao.org/prods/gap/database/gap/files/411_RECOMMENDED_CODE_OF_PRACTICE_FOR_THE_CARE_AND_HANDLING_OF_VEAL_CALVES.HTM>

Canadians for Ethical Treatment of Food Animals. n.d. "About CEFTA." <http://www.cetfa.com/About/tabid/54/Default.aspx>

Canwest News Service. 2008. "Quebec's Labour Day 'Chicken Massacre' Cancelled." August 20. <http://www.canada.com/topics/news/national/story.html?id=a8a18a1c-e50a-4b3e-8201-71eba2de9c71>

Carter, Lee. 2008. "Polar Bears 'At Risk' in Canada." *BBC News*. April 26. <http://news.bbc.co.uk/1/hi/world/americas/7368484.stm>

CBC News. 2008a. "Cat Makes Painful Trip Home, Caught in Leg-Hold Trap." March 17. <http://www.cbc.ca/canada/saskatchewan/story/2008/03/17/saskatchewan-cat.html>

_____. 2008b. "Governments Respond to CBC Report on Horse Slaughter Industry." June 11. <http://www.cbc.ca/canada/saskatchewan/story/2008/06/11/horse-slaughter-reaction.html?ref=rss>

_____. 2009a. "Judge Finds 10 Sealers Guilty of Selling Illegal Pelts." January 27. <http://www.cbc.ca/canada/newfoundland-labrador/story/2009/01/27/blueback-verdict.html>

_____. 2009b. "Veterinarians Train Sealers to Kill Humanely." March 20. <http://www.cbc.ca/canada/newfoundland-labrador/story/2009/03/20/pe-sealers-veterinarians.html>

CBC Radio. 2006. "Horse Meat." *The Current*. <http://www.cbc.ca/thecurrent/2006/200602/20060215.html>

Chandna, Alka. 2009. "Chandna: Stop Animal Abuse at Yale." *Yale Daily News* January 27. <http://www.yaledailynews.com/articles/view/27276>

CIFA. n.d. "Final Report on the National Non-Ambulatory Livestock Consultations." <http://www.inspection.gc.ca/english/anima/

heasan/transport/consultatione.shtml>

Clarke, Ted. 2008. "Children Introduced to Rodeo." *Prince George Citizen*. October 2. <http://www.princegeorgecitizen.com/20081002154464/ sports/sports/children-introduced-to-rodeo.html>

Coronado, Rod. 2000. "Interview with Mirha-Soleil Ross." June 15. *Animal Voices*. (CIUT 89.5FM — Toronto).

Cribb, Robert. 2003. "Meat Processors Cited for Food Safety Violations." *Toronto Star*. September 25. <http://lists.envirolink.org/pipermail/ar-news/Week-of-Mon-20030922/007056.html>

CTV News. 2002. "Raising a Stink." November 15. <http://www.ctv.ca/ servlet/ArticleNews/story/CTVNews/1037381239499_32790439//>

_____. 2003. "Owners of Prison-Run Plant Say Meat Is Safe." October 9.

_____. 2006. "Bizarre BC Cat-Killing Case Extended by One Day." June 30. <http://www.ctv.ca/servlet/ArticleNews/story/ CTVNews/20060630/cat_killer_060630?s_name=&no_ads=>

Daoust, Pierre-Yves, Alice Crook, Trent K. Bollinger, Keith G. Campbell, and James Wong. 2002. "Animal Welfare and the Harp Seal Hunt in Atlantic Canada." *Canadian Veterinary Journal* 43, 9: 687–94.

Davis, Karen. 2005. *The Holocaust and the Henmaid's Tale*. New York: Lantern.

Davis, Mark M. 2008. "A Prescription for Human Immunology." *Immunity Today* 29, 8: 835–38.

Denley, Randall. 2008. "The Humane Society's Big Secret: Euthanasia." *Ottawa Citizen* June 7. <http://www2.canada.com/ottawacitizen/ columnists/story.html?id=296dd806-6505-4f0d-bcdf-3ecf005db18f>

Department of Fisheries and Oceans. 2005. "Seals and Sealing in Canada." Government of Canada. <http://www.dfo-mpo.gc.ca/seal-phoque/ myth_e.htm>

Dion, Stephane. 2008. "April 18, 2008 Statement by the Honourable Stéphane Dion, Leader of the Official Opposition, on the Seal Hunt." Liberal Party of Canada. <http://www.liberal.ca/story_13857_e. aspx>

Donovan, Josephine, and Carol J. Adams (eds.). 2007. *The Feminist Care Tradition in Animal Ethics*. New York: Columbia University Press.

Eaton, Randall. n.d.,a. "Perpetuating Hunter Tradition." <http://www.sci-gg.com/upld/fil/Perpetuating%20Hunter%20Tradition%20by%20 Randall%20Eaton.pdf>

_____. n.d.,b. "The Deer I Never Killed." <http://www.randalleaton.com/ lectures.html>

_____. n.d.,c. "Why We Hunt." <http://www.iwmc.org/IWMC-Forum/RandallEaton/020111-1.htm>

_____. n.d.,d. "Why Hunting is Good Medicine for Youth, Society and the Environment." <http://www.iwmc.org/IWMC-Forum/RandallEaton/030504.doc>

_____. n.d.,e. "Why Hunters Save the World." <http://www.eoni.com/~reaton/articles/Whyhunterssavetheworld.doc>

Edmonton Journal. 2008. "Four Camrose Teens Charged after Cat Microwaved." January 5. <http://www2.canada.com/edmontonjournal/news/story.html?id=13abc91d-cdd9-4323-9ab6-6d9adfe1737b>

Equine Advocates. n.d. "The Premarin (PMU) Industry." <http://www.equineadvocates.com/premarin3.html>

Eshel, Gidon, and Pamela A. Martin. 2006. "Diet, Energy, and Global Warming." *Earth Interactions* 10. Paper Number 9. <http://vancouver-humanesociety.bc.ca/downloads/links/nutriEI.pdf>

Foran, Max. 2008. "The Stampede in Historical Context." In Max Foran (ed.), *Icon, Brand, Myth: The Calgary Exhibition and Stampede.* Edmonton: Athabasca University Press.

Francione, Gary. 1995. *Animals, Property and the Law.* Philadelphia: Temple University Press.

_____. 2000. *Introduction to Animal Rights.* Philadelphia: Temple University.

_____. 2007. "A Bright Spot?" <http://www.abolitionistapproach.com/a-battery-by-any-other-name/>

_____. 2008. "Interview with Gary Francione, Author of Animals as Persons: Essays on the Abolition of Animal Exploitation." Columbia University Press. June 18. <http://www.cupblog.org/?p=283>

_____. 2009. The "Commonplace Reality of Producing Livestock for Consumption." March 22. <http://www.abolitionistapproach.com/>

Friendly Manitoba. n.d. "Eat Local." <http://www.friendlymanitoba.org/eat-local.html>

Fulford, Robert. 2008. "Go Ahead, Take a Bite." *Financial Post* September 8. <http://www.financialpost.com/scripts/story.html?id=b29504ff-3a67-4bd3-9508-ea5cc0db888d&k=17155>

Gelinas, Ben. 2008. "Sentencing Hearing for Teens Who Killed Cat in Microwave." *The Province.* September 5. <http://www2.canada.com/theprovince/news/story.html?id=bd8bd8e6-6964-4b78-84f0-4ef66b2af799>

Global Action Network. n.d. "Fur and Aboriginal People." <http://www.

gan.ca/campaigns/fur+trade/factsheets/fur+and+aboriginal+people.
en.html>

_____. 2007. "2nd Quebec Foie Gras Investigation Overview." <http://
www.gan.ca/campaigns/2nd+quebec+foie+gras+investigation/
overview.en.html>

Government of the Northwest Territories. 2007. *A Survey of American Sports
Hunters who Hunted Polar Bear in NWT in 2007*. Report Prepared for
Industry, Tourism and Investment.

Greek, C. Ray, and Jean Swingle Greek. 2000 *Sacred Cows and Golden Geese:
The Human Cost of Experiments on Animals*. New York: Continuum.

Harding, Katherine. 2007. "Will Canadians Stomach a Horsemeat
Industry?" *Globe and Mail* September 4. <http://www.theglobeand-
mail.com/servlet/story/RTGAM.20070904.whorse04/BNStory/
National/>

Harrison, David. 2007. "We Should Eat Horse Meat, Says Ramsay."
The Telegraph May 7. <http://www.telegraph.co.uk/news/
uknews/1550742/We-should-eat-horse-meat%2C-says-Ramsay.html>

Heberlein, Thomas A., Bjarni Serup and Goran Ericsson. 2008. "Female
Hunting Participation in North America and Europe." *Human Dimensions
of Wildlife* 13: 443–58.

Help Horses. n.d. <http://www3.sympatico.ca/propeller/endslaughter/
qa/qa.htm>. Link is no longer active.

Hinds, Selina. 2008. "Breeding for Bucks." Winnipeg Free Press. September
7. <http://winnipegfreepress.com/special/breedingforbucks/articles/
story/4222721p-4839720c.html>

Hobsbawm, Eric, and Terence Ranger (eds.). 1992. *The Invention of Tradition*.
Cambridge: Cambridge University Press.

Holland, John. 2007. "'Brazen Coup' by Horse Slaughter Company." August
14. <http://tuesdayshorse.wordpress.com/2007/08/14/brazen-coup-
by-horse-slaughter-company/>

Holland, Mark. 2008. "Holland Hopes to Pass Effective Animal Cruelty
Legislation in 40th Parliament." December 1. <http://www.markhol-
land.ca/news/2008/ 120108%20Holland%20hopes%20to%20
pass%20effective%20animal%20cruelty%20legislation%20in%20
the%2040th%20Parliament.htm>

Hollingsworth, Paul. 1990. "Natives and the Fur Industry." *The Peace Newsletter*
October. <http://www.peacecouncil.net/history/PNLs1981-90/
PNL576-1990.pdf>

Horrobin, D.F. 2003. "Modern Biomedical Research: An Internally Self-Consistent Universe with Little Contact with Medical Reality?" *Nature Reviews Drug Discovery* 2: 151–54.

Howden, Saffron, and Vickki Campion. 2007. "Kangaroo's Cruel Canadian Prison." *Daily Telegraph* May 17. <http://www.dailytele-graph.com.au/lifestyle/kangaroos-cruel-canada-prison/story-e6fr-f00i-1111113551565>

Hoyt, John Arthur. 1995. *Animals in Peril*. New York: Avery.

Hribal, Jason. 2003. "'Animals Are Part of the Working Class': A Challenge to Labor History." *Labor History* 44, 4:435–53.

Huang, Lily. 2009. "It's Survival of the Weak and Scrawny." *Newsweek* January 12. <http://www.newsweek.com/id/177709>

Humane Society of the United States. 2005. "American Business Leader Urges Prime Minister To Stop Seal Hunt and Avoid Damage to Canadian Economy." November 5. <http://www.hsus.org/press_and_publications/press_releases/american_business_leader.html

IFAW (International Fund for Animal Welfare). 2008a. "IFAW Hunt Watch 2008: Graphic Video and Accounts of the Hunt." April 2. <http://blog.stopthesealhunt.com/2008/04/ifaw-hunt-watch.html>

_____. 2008b. "Falling Behind." Ottawa: International Fund for Animal Welfare.

International Fur Trade Federation. 2008. "State of the Industry Report." Press Release. <http://www.iftf.com/iftf_3_1_1.php?id=160>

International Vegetarian Union. n.d. "Mohandas K. Gandhi (1869–1948)." <http://www.ivu.org/history/gandhi/>

Jowett, Juliette. 2008. "UN Says Eat Less Meat to Curb Global Warming." *The Observer* September 7. <http://www.guardian.co.uk/environment/2008/sep/07/food.foodanddrink>

Khachatourians, G.G. 1998, "Agricultural Use of Antibiotics and the Evolution and Transfer of Antibiotic-Resistant Bacteria." *Canadian Medical Association Journal* 159, 9: 1129–36.

Kheel, Marti. 1996. "The Killing Game: An Ecofeminist Critique of Hunting." *Journal of the Philosophy of Sport* 23, 1:30–44.

_____. 2008. *Nature Ethics*. Lanham: Rowman and Littlefield.

Knight, Matthew. 2008. "Scientist: Stem Cells Could End Animal Testing." <http://www.cnn.com/2008/HEALTH/12/22/stem.cell.drug.tests/index.html>

Laidlaw, Rob. 2005. *Scales and Tails: The Welfare and Trade of Reptiles Kept as*

Pets in Canada. Toronto: World Society for the Protection of Animals.

Langley, Gill. 2006. *Next of Kin*. London: British Union for the Abolition of Vivisection.

Lapointe, Eugene. 2003. *Embracing the Earth's Wild Resources*. Sherbrooke: Editions du Scribe.

Lavigne, David M. 2005. "Canada's Commercial Seal Hunt is Not "Acceptably Humane." International Fund for Animal Welfare. <www.ifaw.org/Publications/Program_Publications/Seals/asset_upload_file432_12084.pdf ->

Lawrence, Elizabeth Atwood. 1981. *Rodeo*. Chicago: University of Chicago Press.

Laws, Rita. 1994. "Native Americans and Vegetarianism." *Vegetarian Journal*. September. <http://www.ivu.org/history/native_americans.html>

Lee, B.Y., L.G. Hargus, E.J. Webb, A.D. Rickansrud, and C.E. Hagberg. 1979. "Effect of Electrical Stunning on Post Mortem Biochemical Changes and Tenderness in Broiler Breast Muscle." *Journal of Food Science* 44: 1121–22.

Legault, Josee. 2007. "Ducks Suffer So That Gourmets Can Dine." *The Gazette* July 13. <http://www.gan.ca/animal+news.en.html?neid=154>

Leppard, David. 2006. "Elephant Man Drug Victims Told to Expect Early Death." *Times Online* July 30. <http://www.timesonline.co.uk/tol/news/uk/article694634.ece>

Libin, Kevin, 2008. "Killing the Queen's Furry Hats Won't Save the Bears, It Will Just Ruin the Hats." *National Post*. Sepetmber 2. <http://network.nationalpost.com/np/blogs/fullcomment/archive/2008/09/02/kevin-libin-killing-the-queen-s-furry-hats-won-t-save-the-bears-it-will-just-ruin-the-hats.aspx>

Lifton, Robert Jay. 2000. *The Nazi Doctors*. New York: Basic Books.

Loo, Tina. 2006. *States of Nature*. Vancouver: University of British Columbia Press.

Luke, Brian. 2007. *Brutal*. Urbana: University of Illinois.

Mallan, Caroline. 2008. "The Fight Over Foie Gras." *Toronto Star* May 19. <http://www.thestar.com/living/article/427234>

Marketwire. 2008. "Animal Protection Groups Outraged Over Passage of Inadequate Bill." February 15. <www.marketwire.com>

Matthews, Robert. 2008. Medical Progress Depends on Animal Models — Doesn't It? *Journal of the Royal Society of Medicine* 101: 95–98.

Mauser, Gary A. 2004. "Hunters Are the Mainstay of Provincial Wildlife

Management Programs." *Journal of the International Hunter Education Association* Winter: 14.

McBride, Jason. 2007. "One Fine Day." *Toronto Life* May. <http://www.torontolife.com/features/mothers-days/>

McFarlane, B., D. Watson and P. Boxall. 2003. "Women Hunters in Alberta, Canada: Girl Power or Guys in Disguise?" *Human Dimensions of Wildlife* 8, 3:165–80.

Michigan Hunter Recruitment and Retention Work Group. 2006. "Recommendations." January. Lansing: Michigan Department of Natural Resources.

Mills, Andrew. 2005. "Layton Gears Up for Election Fight." *Toronto Star*. September 12. <http://www.nanosresearch.com/news/in_the_news/Toronto%20Star%20September%2012%202005.pdf>

Mitchinson, Paul. 2000. "Calgary Neo-Cons Hunt Controversy." *National Post* July 22. <http://paulmitchinson.com/articles/calgary-school>

Montgomery, Charlotte. 2000. *Blood Relations*. Toronto: Between The Lines.

Montreal Gazette. 2007. "Animal Testing Still Best Option, Researchers Say." June 17.

Moore, Oliver. 2009. "Putin Curbs 'Bloody' Seal Hunt." *Globe and Mail* March 11.

Morrison, Jennifer. 2008. "Battle to Save Horses from Slaughterhouse." *Toronto Star* May 3. <http://www.thestar.com/printArticle/420982>

National Anti-Vivisection Society. n.d. "About NAVS." <http://www.navs.org/site/PageServer?pagename=about_main>

National Institute of Allergy and Infectious Diseases. 1999. "Antimicrobial Fact Sheet." May 4. <http://www.niaid.nih.gov/factsheets/antimicro.htm>

Nibert, David. 2002. *Animal Rights Human Rights*. Lanham: Rowman and Littlefield.

Ontario Veal Association. n.d. "The Appeal Why Choose Ontario Veal." <http://www.ontariovealappeal.ca/choose.php>

Ortega y Gasset, Jose. 1985. *Meditations on Hunting*. New York: Charles Scribner's Sons.

Palmer, Raymond. 2008. "Polar Bear Not Threatened, Canadian Panel Finds." *National Post* April 25. <http://www.nationalpost.com/news/canada/story.html?id=472319>

Patterson, Charles. 2002. *Eternal Treblinka*. New York: Lantern.

Pearson, Craig. 2008. "An Ear for an Ear for Animal Abuser." *Windsor Star*

November 19. <http://www2.canada.com/windsorstar/news/story.html?id=eb154c11-791d-433a-86db-9ab124a64917>

People for the Ethical Treatment of Animals (PETA). n.d.,a. "Suffering in the Wild: The Fur Industry and Indigenous Trappers." <http://www.furisdead.com/indians.asp>

_____. n.d.,b. "Menu Foods Tests Dish Out Cruelty and Suffering." <http://www.peta.org/feat/iams/menu-index.html>

Pet Friendly Canada. 2005. "Newsletter." August. <www.petfriendly.ca/newsletter/2005/05aug.php>

Pew Commission on Industrial Farm Animal Production. 2006. "Putting Meat on the Table: Industrial Farm Animal Production in America." Baltimore: Johns Hopkins Bloomberg School of Public Health.

Poultry Site News. 2009. "Welfare Groups Accuse Canada of Misleading Claims." February 24. <http://www.thepoultrysite.com/poultrynews/17219/welfare-groups-accuse-canada-of-misleading-claims>

Preece, Rod. 1999. *Animals and Nature*. Vancouver: University of British Columbia Press.

Price, Lance B., Elizabeth Johnson, Rocio Vailes, and Ellen Silbergeld. 2005. "Fluoroquinolone-Resistant Campylobacter Isolates from Conventional and Antibiotic-Free Chicken Products." *Environmental Health Perspectives* 113, 5: 557–60.

Psychologists for the Promotion of Animal Welfare. 2006. "Rodeos as Family Entertainment." Media Release. February 6. <http://www.norodeo.org/media/mr-psychologists.htm>

Raincoast Conservation. 2009. "eBay Urged to Halt Sales of Trophy Hunting of Grizzly Bears, Wolves, Cougars." Press Release. Big Wildlife. <http://www.bigwildlife.org/releases_contents.php?id=45>

Regan, Tom. 1983. *The Case for Animal Rights*. Berkeley: University of California.

Rennie, Steve. 2009. "Feds Won't Bar Cat and Dog Fur Imports Because of Seal Ban: Document." Canadian Press. <http://www.google.com/hostednews/canadianpress/article/ALeqM5g0VcHBaKTW2QE4qHhmYmW1TjWeFw>

Ritter, E.M., and M.W. Bowyer. 2005. "Simulation for Trauma and combat Casualty Care." *Minimally Invasive Therapy* 14, 4–5: 224–34.

Robbins, John. 1998. *Diet for a New America*. Novato: New World Library.

_____. 2001. *The Food Revolution*. San Francisco: Conari Press.

Rolfsen, Catherine. 2008. "B.C. Man Guilty of Cruelty For Microwaving

Cat." *Vancouver Sun* May 31. <http://www2.canada.com/vancouver-sun/news/story.html?id=61a8e3ac-a078-4d35-a372-6970109929b3>

Roney, Bruce. 2008. "Euthanasia Is a Task We Loathe." Letter. *Ottawa Citizen* June 11. <http://www2.canada.com/ottawacitizen/news/letters/story.html?id=02230d75-4952-410a-804c-949f0d59d036>

Rowlands, Mark. 2002. *Animals Like Us*. London: Verso

Salt, Henry. 1886. *A Plea for Vegetarianism and Other Essays*. London: Vegetarian Society.

_____. 1894. *Animals Rights Considered in Relation to Social Progress*. New York: Macmillan.

Sanbonmatsu, John. 2004. *The Postmodern Prince*. New York: Monthly Review.

Savlov, Marc. 2004. "That Darn Documentary." *Austin Chronicle* June 24. <http://www.austinchronicle.com/gyrobase/Issue/story?oid=oid%3A276281>

Schiedel, Bonnie. 2001. "Women in the Field." Outdoor Canada. <http://articles.outdoorcanada.ca/homepage/default/women-in-the-field-n257946p1.html>

Sea Shepherd Conservation Society (SSCS). n.d. "Frequently Asked Questions about Canadian Seals and Sealings." <http://www.seashepherd.org/seals/seals-faq.html>

Service B.C. 2005, "British Columbia's Hunting, Trapping & Wildlife Viewing Sector." British Columbia Ministry of Labour and Citizen's Services. August 12. <http://www.bcstats.gov.bc.ca/data/bus_stat/busind/fish/wildlife.pdf>

Sinoski, Kelly. 2008. "Humane Society Invokes Jesus in Rodeo Protest." *Vancouver Sun* July 29.

Smyth, Julie. 2009. "10 Found Guilty of Illegal Sealing." *National Post* January 30. <http://www.harpseals.org/resources/news_and_press/2009/sealhunt09.html>

SPCA of Monterey County. 1999. "Premarin: A Bitter Pill." November/December. <http://www.rare-bird.net/writing/horsepower.html>

Spiegel, Marjorie. 1996. *The Dreaded Comparison*. New York: Mirror.

Stein, Joel. 2007. "Horse — It's What's for Dinner." *Time* February 8. <http://www.time.com/time/magazine/article/0,9171,1587279-1,00.html>

Steinfeld, Henning, Pierre Gerber, Tom Wassenaar, Vincent Castel, Mauricio Rosales, and Cees de Haan. 2006. *Livestock's Long Shadow*. Rome: Food and Agricultural Organization of the United Nations.

Stevens, C.E., C.A. Paszkowski and A.L. Foote. 2007. "Beaver (Castor Canadensis) as a Surrogate Species for Conserving Anuran Amphibians on Boreal Streams in Alberta, Canada." *Biological Conservation* 134, 1 (January): 1–13.

Sunday Times. 2007. "Foie Gras Could be Tasty Way to Get Alzheimer's." June 17. <www.timesonline.co.uk/tol/news/uk/health/article1942949>

Sztybel, David. n.d. "The Canadian Council on Animal Care's Code of Ethics: A Critical Evaluation." Medical Research Modernization Committee. <http://www.mrmcmed.org/DavidSztybel.html>

Taylor, Bill. 2007. "Looking for Exotic Animals? Tigers Are Cheap, Roos Costly." *Toronto Star* May 24. <http://www.thestar.com/News/article/217206>

_____. 2008. "Yee-haw, the Rodeo's Back!" *Toronto Star* August 8 <http://www.thestar.com/article/473346>

Teitel, Murray. 2008. "The Millions Ottawa Spends Subsidizing the Seal Hunt. *National Post* April 17. <http://network.nationalpost.com/np/blogs/fpcomment/archive/tags/Murray+Teitel/default.aspx>

Tesher, Ellie. 2001. "Animal Rights Fanatics Are Health Hazard." *Toronto Star* October 16. <http://archives.foodsafety.ksu.edu/animalnet/2001/10-2001/animalnet_october_16.htm>

Troutman, Dorrinda. 2008. "Horse Processing in Canada." *Rocky Mountain Rider* May. <http://www.rockymountainrider.com/articles/0508_horse_processing_canada.htm>

Ubyssey. 2008. "Cruel Intentions? Animal experimentation at UBC." January 25. <http://ubyssey.bc.ca/2008/01/25/cruel-intentions-animal-experimentation-at-ubc/>

United Nations Food and Agricultural Organization. 2006. "Livestock a Major Threat to Environment." November 29. <http://www.fao.org/newsroom/en/news/2006/1000448/index.html>

United Poultry Concerns. 2005. "Humaneness of Killing Birds with Carbon Dioxide Is Disputed by Science." Press release. <http://www.upc-online.org/nr/33005co2.htm>

Vallis, Mary. 2008. "Horse Lobby Presses for Slaughter Ban." *National Post* January 26. <http://portal.sre.gob.mx/canada/pdf/horselobby28.pdf>

Vancouver Sun. 2007. "Dog-fight Rings Tough to Crack in B.C." August 23. <http://www.canada.com/story_print.html?id=801757ba-a7f6-4718-a214-e04dfe489653&sponsor=>

Vegan Society. n.d. "Land." <http://www.vegansociety.com/environment/land/>

Vidal, John. 2004. "Wildlife Trade? It's a Jungle Out There." *Guardian* September 30. <http://www.guardian.co.uk/print/0,3858,5027213-111414,00.html>

Walker, Polly, Pamela Rhubart-Berg, Shawn McKenzie, Kristin Kelling, and Robert S Lawrence. 2005. "Public Health Implications of Meat Production and Consumption." (Invited Paper.) *Public Health Nutrition* 8, 4: 348–56

Wetherell, Donald G. 2008. "Making Tradition: The Calgary Stampede 1912–1959." In Max Foran (ed.), *Icon, Brand, Myth: The Calgary Exhibition and Stampede*. Edmonton: Athabasca University Press.

Wiecek, Paul. 2006. "Saddling Up For Slaughter." *Winnipeg Free Press* September 17. <http://www.fund4horses.org/info.php?id=847>

Wingrove, Josh. 2009. "SPCA Vows to Pursue Charges in Case of Starving Horses." *Globe and Mail* March 17. <http://www.theglobeandmail.com/servlet/story/LAC.20090317.BCHORSES17/TPStory/National>

World Watch Institute. 2004. "Is Meat Sustainable?" *World Watch Magazine* 17, 4 (July/August). <http://www.worldwatch.org/node/549>

Worthington, Peter. 2008. "Why Do They Call This Slaughter a 'Hunt'?" *National Post* April 17.

Useful Websites

Animal Voices Radio Archive <http://www.animalvoices.ca/shows>
"Toronto's animal liberation radio show broadcasting locally on CIUT 89.5 FM and worldwide at www.ciut.fm, live, every Tuesday at 11 am-noon EST. Volunteer-run, Animal Voices covers the local, national, global, and politically diverse campaigns, struggles and victories of the animal liberation movement."

Animal Alliance <http://www.animalalliance.ca/index.html>
"Committed to the protection of all animals and the promotion of a harmonious relationship among people, animals and the environment."

Ark-II <http://www.ark-ii.com/2009/>
"Toronto-based, grassroots animal advocacy organization. ARK II organizes and hosts events in and around the Toronto area on a broad range of issues including: farmed animals; veganism; animals used for textiles, in-

cluding leather, fur, and wool; animals used in laboratories; hunting and fishing; and companion animals, including strays and over-breeding."

Fur-Bearer Defenders <http://www.banlegholdtraps.com/home_parent.htm> "Non-profit society working to stop trapping cruelty and protect fur-bearing animals."

Global Action Network <http://www.gan.ca/home.en.html> "Nationally incorporated non-profit organization, dedicated to fostering environmental awareness and action. We believe that animals, the environment, and human welfare are inextricably linked. Simply put, animal abuse and the destruction of our environment has an ultimate consequence — the degradation of the human species."

Lifeforce <http://www.lifeforcefoundation.org/index.php> "Non-profit Vancouver based ecology organization that was formed in 1981 to raise public awareness of the interrelationship between people, animals, and the environment. We promote animal rights and ecological responsibility. In order to develop a non-violent society we must extend our circle of compassion to include all sentient creatures with whom we share this planet."

Niagara Action for Animals <http://niagaraactionforanimals.org/> "To advocate for all animals through education and community outreach. We envision a compassionate society that respects the innate worth of all animals. Niagara Action For Animals (NAfA) is an all-volunteer, registered charity."

Liberation BC <http://liberationbc.org/> "Vancouver-based animal rights organization dedicated to liberating animals through education, outreach and advocacy. We stand by our actions and engage in our activism in our own names and with our faces showing. We promote a vegan lifestyle and an end to all exploitation of animals."

Vancouver Humane Society <http://www.vancouverhumanesociety.bc.ca/home> "Registered charity dedicated to the humane treatment of animals. We encourage individuals, organizations, and governments to take responsibility for the welfare and rights of domestic animals and wildlife influenced by human activities."

Zoocheck Canada <http://www.zoocheck.com/about.html>
  "National animal protection charity... established in 1984 to promote and protect the interests and well-being of wild animals. For more than 20 years, Zoocheck has been a leading voice for the protection of wild animals. We are the only Canadian organization with a specific focus on captive wild animal issues and problems."